Cats in Charge

Cats in Charge

A Siamese Saga in the West Country

Philip Lawrence

Matador
9 Priory Business Park
Kibworth Beauchamp
Leicestershire LE8 0RX, UK
Tel: (+44) 116 279 2299
Fax: (+44) 116 279 2277
Email: books@troubador.co.uk
Web: www.troubador.co.uk/matador

ISBN 978 1784620 189

British Library Cataloguing in Publication Data.
A catalogue record for this book is available from the British Library.

Typeset in Aldine401 BT Roman by Troubador Publishing Ltd
Printed and bound in the UK by TJ International, Padstow, Cornwall

Matador is an imprint of Troubador Publishing Ltd

This book is dedicated to the memory of
Doreen and René Tovey

Contents

"The smallest feline is a masterpiece"

- Leonardo da Vinci

Preface

My wife and I are huge fans of the cat books written by Doreen Tovey. Doreen, a former President of the Siamese Cat Club, was from Bristol, but lived for many years in a cottage in a small valley on the edge of the village of Rowberrow, near Winscombe in Somerset. Having acquired a Siamese queen and then subsequently two of her kittens, ostensibly to deal with invading mice, Doreen and her husband, René (called Charles in the books) were soon hooked on the oriental felines and Doreen began to write what became a series of some 14 books concerning the antics of the cats and a number of typical Somerset characters that lived in or near Rowberrow.

The books, which are utterly charming and imbued with great wit, became popular worldwide and for some time Doreen was a very well known writer, appearing on both TV and Radio. But, of course memory soon fades, and despite more recent reprints in paperback, far fewer people have heard of Doreen today. Sadly she

Doreen Tovey's lovely white cottage in Rowberrow. Now sadly a wreck and ripe for redevelopment.

died back in 2008 and the famous white cottage, where the various Siamese twosomes lived, is now empty and semi-derelict.

The short book that follows is a tribute to Doreen and her work. But not written in the same style and in no way meant to mimic Doreen Tovey's work, which was quite unique. The author of this work about three Siamese lives just a few miles from Rowberrow and often goes down with his wife, Benita, to look at the cottage and imagine the antics of Solomon and Sheba and the various successors that lived there from the 1950s. The spirit, and indeed the ashes of Doreen and those of the cats, inhabit the quiet valley where they all found happiness together. Long may they be remembered.

The first chapter that follows will introduce new readers to Doreen Tovey's life and work and hopefully explain the logic underpinning this book. I hope that for those who are already familiar with the books, it will rekindle some pleasant memories and also perhaps trigger the odd smile or humorous recollection.

Doreen Tovey's Legacy

Biography

Doreen Tovey (Dorean on her birth certificate) was born in Bristol in October 1918, just after the end of the First World War. Tragically, just two weeks after Doreen's birth, her mother Miriam Mizen (nee Burge) died at the age of 26 in the flu pandemic of that year and she was brought up by her grandmother, Rhoda Mizen. Mrs Rhoda Mizen's maiden name was Weare and her mother, Ann Weare, had lived with her husband sheep farming in Argentina, before coming to Bristol in the late 19th century. Rhoda Mizen (Weare) had one daughter, who Doreen Tovey refers to as Louisa in her books, but in fact Louisa was her middle name and this woman was called Violet.

After her mother died Doreen lived with Rhoda Mizen and her daughter Violet (Louisa in the books) and the book *Life with Grandma* relates the life and experiences that Doreen Tovey had with her grandmother in a house in Milford Street at Southville in Bristol. The property, a handsome three storey terrace, is still standing and in good order today. For those interested in more information about Doreen Tovey's life, some other additional details about the early period in Bristol can be found in *Roses Round the Door*, published in 1982 by Michael Joseph.

Doreen's father, Frederick, was one of Rhoda Mizen's 5 sons. In some of her books Doreen Tovey mentions "father" working away in far flung places as an engineer. He seems to have had very little role in Doreen's life. Her early years were carefully policed by "Grandma", who had strong views about what was appropriate for a young lady's conduct. In *Life with Grandma* we get a glimpse of a happy childhood, albeit at times a rather eccentric one. One thing that is clear is that Grandma's menagerie of animals was a strong influence on Doreen Tovey's love of flora and fauna and also in a tendency she had to put the interests of animals before those of humans. Rhoda Mizen appears to have been fiercely protective of her parrots and other exotic pets, including an owl called Gladstone that used to perch on the top of the bathroom door watching, while members of the household performed their ablutions. Grandma was prone to rescue any lost animals that needed succour and believed that people were better able to look after themselves. Mrs Mizen was certainly what today we would call a "character" and wont to visit Doreen's school to impart advice to any teachers that were treating her granddaughter in ways that she disapproved of.

Another key person in Doreen Tovey's life was Rhoda Mizen's daughter, Violet. Doreen Tovey's aunt Violet appears to have been a great friend and confidant to her and the books relate many amusing tales about Violet and Doreen's adventures. In *Life with Grandma* Doreen tells the story of a visit with Violet to a wedding in a village in North Somerset. In the narrative she seems very enamoured of the countryside and the village way of life, although also conscious of the hardship and the discipline necessary in farming communities. Nevertheless, it is clear that the seeds were sown for a yearning to live away from Bristol in Somerset and engage in country pursuits.

After primary school Doreen Tovey attended grammar school in Bristol, but for financial reasons was unable to go on to university, as she had hoped. After grammar school she worked at a couple of clerical jobs and then joined Imperial Tobacco in Bristol, first as a typist and later a secretary, just prior to the outbreak of war in 1939. At Imperial Tobacco the management became aware of Doreen's talents as a writer and she was moved into the public relations' department, where her literary skills could be put to good use. Ultimately, after the war, she was given the job of statistical librarian, writing reports and papers that were reviewed at board level. As she herself commented this was a significant and unusual promotion for a woman at that time.

While working at Imperial Tobacco, Doreen Tovey met her future husband, René Carl Daniel Tovey, who worked in the accounts' department. Allegedly they just happened to bump into each other on a flight of stairs. René was born in Canada in 1913 and was the son of William Matthews Tovey, who was born in 1882, probably in Bristol and was an only child. René had a younger brother, Eric William Tovey, also born in Bristol in 1920. Eric is mentioned only rarely by Doreen, but crops up a couple of times in *Roses Round the Door.*

In the famous cat books Doreen calls her husband Charles, possibly to ward off the idea that he was a Frenchman. Certainly René does not sound very convincing for the name of a West Country man pursuing a traditional village life in Somerset. Generally, most of the characters in the books have pseudonyms, but, just to make the researcher's job a little more difficult, not all.

Trials and tribulations

Reading Doreen Tovey's personal diaries, which one of her closest old friends has kindly let me see, it's clear that true love did not always run smoothly for Doreen and René. In the diaries Doreen offers some trenchant complaints about René not turning up for dates and their lack of a proper social life. Doubtless courtship was ever so. But navigating around the intrusions of Grandma must also have been difficult. Indeed, Rhoda Mizen had already scared off a young clergyman who had taken a shine to aunt Violet, who remained a spinster throughout her life, like so many women after the First World War.

As this was in the late 1930s the shadow of the Second World War was also looming over the couple and René was called up for service with the Royal Navy. Reading the diaries it is clear that by this time Doreen had a deep yearning for an independent life with

René and away from Grandma. And during a brief leave for René, prior to his embarkation (sailing overseas) in December 1940, the couple were hastily married by special licence in a church that Doreen refers to as St. Paul's in Bristol. The couple thought that they were very fortunate. For when Doreen went to obtain the licence she was told that the church had been bombed out. But to their relief, Doreen and René found that it was still standing, despite the fact that the surrounding area was a desolate bomb site. After their rushed nuptials, the newlyweds spent a brief honeymoon at a Somerset farmhouse and then René went off to war in the Middle East.

With René thousands of miles away in Egypt, Doreen Tovey threw herself into her work and supporting the war effort. As well as working full time she joined the Red Cross and also the Voluntary Aid Detachment (VAD) organisation, whose nurses supplemented the efforts of military medical staff. After just 50 hours training Doreen Tovey was helping to nurse wounded servicemen in Bristol. It is also clear from her books that during this difficult period her bond and dependence on her aunt increased and that she and Violet were great friends. Doreen appears to have spent most of her spare time with her beloved aunt.

After two and a half lonely years René came back home from the Middle East and, to Doreen's delight, following a period of training in London, he was given a shore posting back in the South West. But the life in a dream cottage that Doreen sought to share with René was still not to be. In 1943 René's father, William, had died and she and René moved in with Rene's mother for two years; not every new bride's greatest wish. After this Doreen and René rented a number of properties in the countryside around Bristol, including a wing of a large house at Dundry, just a few miles to the south of Bristol, but perched 700 feet up on a steep hill with terrific views of the Somerset countryside. The house was owned by a wealthy Dundry businessman who was not universally popular in the village. Doreen relates a number of amusing tales about him *in Roses Round the Door,* including the villagers burning of him in effigy on V.E. night in May

4

1945. Doreen and René must have been at this house in the severe winter of 1946/47, as she writes of being marooned in her "hill village", with René unable to get his car up the steep slopes.

Shortly after this stay in Dundry, where Doreen thought the "hill village" people a "little odd", the Toveys found their dream cottage at Rowberrow, near Churchill on the A38. Rowberrow has a steep lane next to the village pub that goes down to a small valley with a few houses built hard up against the hillside. A small stream runs along the valley floor and Doreen and René Tovey's cottage was the first property at the bottom of the lane on the left, just across on the far side of the stream. The property came complete with a couple of acres of land, which was perfect for grazing the Tovey's beloved donkey, Annabel. This is where Doreen and René settled in with their menagerie and Doreen began to write her series of well known cat books. Altogether Doreen Tovey wrote 14 books, 8 of which were predominantly about the cats. In total her books sold more than 120,000 copies worldwide. She had many ardent fans from around the world who corresponded with her at the White Cottage. Some readers would even turn up on the doorstep and demand to meet the famous cats.

Doreen Tovey's cats

The books about cats began with *Cats in the Belfry*, published in 1957. The final cat book was *Cats in Concord* (2001). As the dates reveal they span over four decades. *Cats in the Belfry* is a delightful book, enlivened by the freshness and intensity of Doreen's feelings for the cats. It describes the Tovey's first Siamese experience with the female blue point Sugieh and then two of her kittens, Solomon and Sheba. Sadly, Sugieh died at the age of four after being spayed, which back then was a much more risky procedure than today. Early in the book Doreen admits that she was not really a great cat enthusiast to begin with and, in fact, Sugieh was only acquired to eliminate some troublesome mice, who were a legacy of the Tovey's pet squirrel,

Blondin. The mice were attracted to the store of nuts and other food stuffs that Blondin hid in the cottage. But according to Doreen, they turned rather truculent after poor Blondin's demise when the food store disappeared. As one might expect from a contrary Siamese, Sugieh ignored the mice completely and pursued her own agenda bringing havoc to the Tovey household.

In *Cats in the Belfry* Doreen Tovey introduces the reader to some of the typical Somerset country characters in her village. This is a very effective device, as it breaks up the narrative about the cats and gives the book a wider frame of reference in relation to village life. She writes with great humour and affection about these characters and manages to weave the antics of the cats into the wider story about the village principals. One such individual is Father Adams, not a clergyman, but rather the head of a farm labourer's household down the lane from the Tovey's cottage. In the first book we learn that Father Adams has become the proud owner of a female Siamese called Mimi ((pronounced Mymy by our bucolic yeoman). Adams thinks that Mimi is going to make him a small fortune by providing litters of exquisite and expensive kittens. But he hasn't bargained for the calls of a female Siamese queen when they require a mate. Mimi screams the place down and drives all concerned around the bend. Father Adams's plans end in tears and Doreen Tovey also realises that being a breeder is no picnic.

The narrative in *Cats in the Belfry* also relates Charles's (René's) hapless attempts to do some DIY at the cottage. At times it reads like some of the slap stick scenes from the 1970s Michael Crawford BBC sitcom, *Some Mothers Do 'Ave Em"*. The cats are at the heart of these disasters, falling into ponds and drains, getting covered in soot and even being plastered in blue paint on one occasion. In one episode Solomon gets inside a grandfather clock with disastrous results. This is all great fun and offers a nice mix of slapstick and irony. Gradually, in later books, other stock in trade characters are introduced, such as the odd job man Fred Ferry, the Rector and an eccentric old lady called Miss Wellington.

The first publisher that took on Doreen's books was Michael

6

Joseph. Mr Joseph, a very prominent publisher, read the manuscript of *Cats in the Belfry* himself and was enchanted by it. He was not alone; some years later the writer Jilly Cooper also became a big fan. She described *Cats in the Belfry* as, 'The most enchanting cat book ever'. This heavyweight support is not surprising. These books are not the typical fare served up in sentimental animal/pet story writing. The style is witty and elegant and the classical and historical references elevate the books to a higher level than the normal writing about pets. Of course it helps if you are a cat lover; for feline fans these books are pure nectar. A rich and enchanting draught of pure fun and delight.

Sheba and Solomon crop up again in *Cats in May*, published in 1959 by Elek books. Here Doreen describes the cats' appearance on a BBC Television programme, during which Solomon, in particular,

Cat lovers everywhere are indebted to Summersdale publishers for re-printing some of the books in paperback over the last decade or so.

wreaks havoc and causes utter chaos in the studio. They get back to Somerset utterly frazzled and Charles, feeling humiliated, vows never again! Beginning with this episode the books now introduce a compelling new idea; the Toveys are depicted as going slowly bonkers under the influence of the cats. The cats terrify the Rector, scare Aunt Ethel out of her wits, undermine the efforts of Sidney the gardener and make Charles a laughing stock in the village. It is all great fun.

This was a period of great productivity and success for Doreen Tovey and the adventures of Solomon and Sheba appeared in print in the US, with *Cats in May* re-titled as *Cats in Cahoots* for American readers in 1960. At this time Doreen was using the artist Maurice Wilson as her illustrator and the drawings in *Cats in Cahoots* are particularly splendid. He captures the Siamese look perfectly and his originals, which I have seen, are worthy pieces of art in themselves.

Cats in May is remarkable as, although it is difficult to upstage a Siamese, arguably this is achieved in the book by the Tovey's pet squirrel, Blondin. Blondin, who the Toveys adopted as a baby after he fell out of a dray in the top of a fir tree, eats his way through a fair bit of the Tovey's furniture. But he is a civilised little fellow and he always joins Charles and Doreen for a cup of tea at breakfast time. He also aroused great concern at Imperial Tobacco, during a phase when Doreen took the little blighter with her to work. One day, partly for self preservation, Charles and Doreen decide to return Blondin to the wild. They place him in the nearby woods at the foot of a fir tree, where there is a dray. But their furry friend is having none of it. When they place him at the foot of the tree, he turns 180 degrees and bounds full tilt back to the cottage. The bed and board is just too good. Doreen remarks that Blondin 'has really got to her' Charles replies,' I think we got to him too'.

After the death of Solomon the Toveys acquired Seeley, whose adventures are outlined in the *New Boy*, published by Elek books in 1970. Doreen Tovey was quite besotted with Solomon and her reaction to his death is very moving at the beginning of the new book. Seeley then arrives and has a lot to live up to, but he meets the challenge very well. Indeed, I have to confess that he is my favourite of Doreen's cats. Showing that he understands the great Tovey Siamese tradition he falls into the fishpond on his second day at the White Cottage. The book describes more of Seeley's misadventures, including him being bitten by an adder and his propensity to run off and get lost. He is a most disaster prone male.

Two years later in 1972 *Double Trouble* introduces Shebalu, after Sheba' s death at 16 years of age. This charming book relates a very happy period in the Tovey's life. Everyone is in good health and Doreen and Charles are very much at the centre of life in Rowberrow. Charles is clearly smitten with Shebalu and, as with Sheba before, she is very much a Daddy's girl. It is also clear that Doreen adores Seeley, despite his penchant for courting disaster. The Toveys never had children and it's clear that the cats, and Annabel the donkey, were, in effect, their substitute family. In *Double Trouble* the reader also learns more about village characters such as Father Adams and the hapless builder Henry. We are also introduced to Miss Wellington, an eccentric spinster who tears up and down the A38 on her electric scooter. It is a very joyful and amusing book.

In the next book the mood changes very starkly. Disaster strikes in the *Coming of Saska* in 1977, as the beloved Seeley disappears, never to be found again. The book details the frantic efforts that the Toveys made to find Seeley, but not the real pain they must have felt on his loss. Doreen does not really cry on our sleeve. But it must have been a terrible experience; much worse that finding a body to bury and mourn. It was suspected that Seeley might have been stolen, or perhaps taken by a fox, but the disappearance remained a sad and troubling mystery. But life goes on and after Seeley, Saska, who came from my breeder friend Pauline Furber, arrives at the White Cottage. Saska continued the tradition of bonkers male Siamese who are always getting into trouble and arousing the curiosity of the village community when Doreen has to go to the rescue.

Around this time the Canadian Government invited Doreen and René on a trip to the Rocky Mountains to observe and write about

Canadian wildlife, with a special focus on Grizzly Bears. This trip is detailed in *The Coming of Saska*. When Doreen tells Father Adams about the trip he foresees disaster and when the Toveys see their first Grizzly they discover that they have locked themselves out of their motor home. Doreen fears that she and René are about to become the bear's supper. But contrary to Father Adams dire forecast, Doreen and René survive to recount their adventures.

Undoubtedly, one of the best of Doreen Tovey's works is *A Comfort of Cats* published in 1980. This gives more detail about Saska and village characters such as Father Adams, Fred Ferry and a new couple called the Bannetts. It is revealed that Saska is a very able retriever and is seen by villagers bringing sticks and other objects back to the Toveys on the lawn of the cottage. Fred Ferry, handyman come poacher, thinks that they could 'half train he to be useful'. In fact, retrieving is not uncommon in Siamese, who are often said to have dog like characteristics. Certainly they like to share in the full domestic life of the household and become accustomed to certain set routines. Doreen tells the reader that her cats like to go to bed at a certain time and do not like visitors to stay too late.

The comedic high point of *A Comfort of Cats* revolves around the Toveys acquiring a caravan. During the summer they do three trips in the van and then begin ruminating on whether the Siamese duo can join the household on tour. Charles decides that a few practice runs would be useful, so the Toveys experiment by moving into the caravan with the cats. They want to keep this dark, but Fred Ferry spots them and spills the beans to the rest of the village. To make matters worse, Doreen finds that Saska and Shebalu will not give them any peace when they have a meal. So the two naughty Siamese are locked in the car. Subsequently, a steady stream of villagers decide to take evening walks down in the valley to see what the mad Toveys are up to. As three farm labourers approach Doreen and Charles throw themselves onto the caravan floor to try and evade detection. They hear one of the men comment, 'Cracked... have been for years'.

A Change of direction

Very sadly, shortly after *A Comfort of Cats* was published René Tovey died of a massive heart attack. Things were never the same again, neither in the books nor in life. Doreen subsequently lived by herself for the best part of 30 years. Not long after René's death she published *Waiting in the Wings*, which did not appeal to all of her readers. The book is heavily influenced by a belief in the afterlife and spiritualism. Doreen tells the reader that Charles is still with her and guiding her through the challenges of life. In some other books she mentions potential suitors who would like to marry her, but she stays true to Charles's memory. The book has some sad motifs, including the difficult question of how single women rebuild their social lives after bereavement. Doreen believes that some of her old friends avoid her now that she is a widow.

Only two more cat book follows in the subsequent decades, *More Cats in the Belfry*, published in 1995 and *Cats in Concord*, published in 2001. *More Cats in the Belfry* deepens the characterisation of figures like Fred Ferry, the handyman and the village eccentric, Miss Wellington, who drives her disability scooter in reckless fashion along the main roads to Luscombe (Winscombe). Saska is still alive and well, but now partnered by a new girl, called Tani. The latter book tells the tale of Rama and Tani; it is also a charming book, but perhaps not quite in the same rank as some of the earlier works. There is one wonderful moment where Doreen relates meeting a formidable male Siamese called Ming. She asks the reader, rhetorically, if calling a Siamese after a Chinese emperor was really a good idea?

Sadly, by this time Doreen was severely incapacitated by arthritis, but still insisted on using her old typewriter. The lack of output in the later years partly reflected this limitation, but also the fact that many of the central and lovable characters that she wrote about were gone. She died in January 2008. The White Cottage was bought at auction for redevelopment, but remains intact at the time of writing, bowed but not broken.

2

The Year of the Cat

My own Siamese cat odyssey was also, like Doreen Tovey's, delayed well into adulthood. The following narrative relates my experience in coming to a point in life when, as the Toveys were, one is driven barmy by Siamese cats. But the addiction to these seductive, beautiful and mischievous animals is hard to shake off. Be careful of what you wish for, especially if it is a feline that comes from the kingdom of Siam.

Cats at bay

As a child I had always wanted a cat. But when growing up my family had often moved house and were quite unsettled. Also my father, brought up in the countryside in the early 1900s, had a typically hard bitten attitude to animals, especially those not perceived to be useful. I did smuggle a kitten home once from a farm where I had been sent on an "outward bound" style holiday. But it only remained with us a few days before it was re-homed. Neither I, nor the lovely ginger kitten, had been particularly welcome when I returned from my little adventure on the farm. No cats for me!

My desire to possess a feline pal was also thwarted by my first wife, who like my father, was not really an animal lover. It's amazing what you miss when you are falling in love. The Lawrence household was clean and tidy, but not one adorned, or inconvenienced, by the presence of a pet. After my sons were born a process of negotiation resulted in the arrival of a goldfish. But my relationship with Joey lacked something. Attempts to get close were thwarted, cuddles were tricky and, contrary to the old feminist joke, fish are often busy training on their bicycles. Generally, my relationship with Joey was formal, unemotional and stilted. I am not a pescephile.

Some years later I thought I had secured a little feline pal. I was out jogging in the local countryside on a lovely May evening, when I heard a tiny, squeaky miaow coming from behind a hedge running along a local farmer's field. Investigation revealed a small, black and white kitten cowering under the hedge row and calling for his mum. He was miles from anywhere and I believe the poor little chap had just been dumped. I picked him up and jogged back home at a good pace as I was determined to convince my wife that fate had sent this furry gift to the Lawrence household. But no luck again. He disappeared behind the fridge and I never saw him again. He was soon adopted by one of my wife's colleagues at her school. Fortunately, he did go on to enjoy a long and happy life and I suppose it's no good staying where you are not welcome. Even Kismet could not give me a cat.

Be Lucky!

But change rules our lives and after a rather difficult period for me, when I experienced the failure of my marriage and a divorce from my first wife, I found that I had more control over how I wanted to live and the possibility of a feline friend became more likely. But my new partner and I were living in a rented flat, which wasn't ideal as a home for a cat and indeed pet ownership was not permitted by the landlord. Nevertheless, back in the early 1990s, while lecturing at Swansea University, my girlfriend (Benita) and I acquired a cross-Siamese from a lady who was going to move in with her son, where there was a male Rottweiler. Lucky, as he was known, had not lived up to his name and was not part of the deal, so a local Newsagent's window sported an advertisement for a *"Siamese cross-breed, very friendly and affectionate and free to a good home"*.

 13

Within an hour of me seeing the advertisement, my two sons, James and Alex, and I were round at the house of the lady who owned the cat. Having chased Lucky around the lady's residence for two hours we eventually got him into a cat box provided by his mistress. It was clear that she loved him very much and was going to miss him. But she didn't want him terrorising by a Rottweiler and she seemed to regard us as offering the prospect of a good new home. But then, just as she was making some tea to settle our nerves, Lucky broke out of the cat box and the whole palaver of pursuing him around the house began again. And by the way, cat owners should beware of plastic cat boxes, as big strong males can smash the doors open. These days our three Siamese escape artists are carted about in a cage that would not be out of place at Pentonville or Parkhurst prison. There must be a Siamese somewhere called Houdini!

Lucky, evading us with the skill of the Scarlet Pimpernel, did not want to go back into his cat cage. And it was another hour or so before the feline escapologist was finally re-captured and put in the boot of my car to be transported to my flat. On arrival he was terrified and disappeared under the bed in the spare room for two days. I had telephoned my girlfriend to say that we now had a cat. She was delighted, but furious that I had put him in the boot of the car. Unfortunately, I had heard a vet on a radio show suggesting that placing an animal, that was moving house, in a dark place would reduce the disorientation for the poor itinerant. Benita was not impressed and suggested we might try the tactic on the vet, or maybe me. She was also somewhat apprehensive, as the flat was not the best environment for an "entire" male cat. She left work early and returned home to take charge.

After a couple of days coaxing, Benita finally managed to make Lucky show himself and she was able to see that we had gained a handsome and muscular black cat who looked somewhat Siamese. Apparently, for genetic reasons, Siamese half-breeds are always black. Lucky was the result of an unintended mating between a seal point pedigree queen and a local moggie bruiser who had spotted

14

Lucky, or Mr. Luxman as he was later known, luxuriating on the Axminster carpet in the living room. Siamese, even crossed, love comfort and luxury.

the Thai beauty in his owner's back garden. The seal point queen's breeder kept the cat indoors, but, as sometimes happens, the urge to mate had prompted her escape to find an available, but in this case, unwelcome suitor. Lucky and four other black furry bundles were the progeny. Lucky had then gone to live with a neighbour of the breeder until the prospect of a house share with the Rottweiler loomed. The Lawrence's came riding to the rescue, but had a lot to learn about Siamese cats.

It was very quickly apparent to us that we had found an adorable pet. Lucky was gentle, vocal, funny, friendly and a great companion. The one point of vexation was that, as he was un-neutered, he was desperate to get out and find some female company. This meant head butting the windows at night and calling to any available feline

15

ladies. He also began to spray; one of the great problems of indoor cats, especially entire males. Fortunately this did not get out of hand, but even a small amount of spray creates a terrible stink and proved another incentive to find a house and garden so that Lucky could go out and seek his true love. In fact, we had already been thinking about a move to a bigger property. Within two months we had found a large semi-detached Victorian house in Sketty, overlooking Swansea bay. The house had a decent sized rear garden and the local traffic was fairly light. Next door, a property owned by a Labour councillor, had fallen into disrepair and had a somewhat overgrown back garden; this would not have appealed to Hyacinth Bucket, but was a perfect playground for our new feline friend. In December 1993, on a horrible wet day, the three of us moved into our new home, which was just 500 yards up the road. After a couple of days, and much fretting and trepidation, Lucky was allowed to go out, but not before about one pound of butter had been spread on his paws. He slid, rather than walked down the path to his new found freedom. In the meantime we had also had him neutered and discovered that he was about 18 months old. All was set fair for domestic bliss with our new half-Siamese friend.

Attitudes to Siamese

We were very proud about having acquired Lucky, as even a half Siamese seemed quite posh to us. We immediately told a number of our friends and colleagues that we had found ourselves a cat and it turned out, rather to our surprise, that quite a few people in our social circle had strong views on Siamese. The message we got was that this was not a breed to be trifled with and that we had been very sensible not to go the whole hog and acquire a pedigree. The idea seemed to be that a cross-breed had some of the typical intelligence and savoir-faire of the Siamese, but not the full gamut of mischief making and the ability to wreak havoc for which, post Disney's *Lady and the Tramp*, Siamese were famous. Our solicitor pal Doug; a big, bluff, no-nonsense ex-rugby player type, explained to us how his neighbour's Siamese were always getting into his house and stealing food. He told us how he had bought a powerful water pistol and soaked the two culprits so thoroughly that they had disappeared up his chimney in terror. At the time I remember being shocked and thinking that this seemed too aggressive and typically moronic "rugger bugger" male behaviour. But if someone related such a story to me now, rugby player or not, I would simply punch them on the nose and ring the RSPCA. Yes, I have to confess; I gave up British nationality and became a citizen of the feline kingdom of Siam long ago.

Our macho legal friend's views were correct in one respect, Lucky was different to a typical moggie. Generally more slim-line and with a long aquiline nose and big ears. Especially side-on, his profile looked very seal point and he chatted away all the time in the typical Siamese manner. He also retrieved objects that were thrown for him and in many ways was quite dog like. But even a half-Siamese has his foibles. Lucky did not like visitors coming to our house. If someone knocked at the door or rang the bell he would growl like an angry lion, as though he would go for the jugular as soon as the caller crossed the threshold. But actually he was really a big softy and when anyone entered the house he would dart under a sideboard or bed. He also hated being transported by car and when this occurred he would make a noise that would awaken the dead. It was a loud and modulated deep-throated wail, with a mixture of anger and terror thrown in for good measure. Benita could barely stand to listen to it for even 5 minutes and was horror struck when trips to the vet were necessary.

As mentioned in chapter one Doreen Tovey called one of her books *A Comfort of Cats*. It's a beautiful title and also most appropriate for the joy of owning a good natured cat. On cold winter evenings, in our living room overlooking Swansea bay, Lucky would stretch out in front of the fire and wriggle about on his back, looking the picture of contentment. We would be snuggled up on the sofa, either watching TV or listening to some music. It was a simple, but utterly blissful experience, especially after a hard week at work. At this time my poor partner, Benita, was travelling everyday to her job in Bristol, which meant getting up at 5:30am and then catching the 6:32am train from Swansea. I normally took Benita to the station and then returned home to get an early start on my work. I would be at my desk upstairs in the study and Lucky would come and sit on my lap and help me write lecture notes.

Absence makes the heart grow fonder

As we got settled into our new regime there was only one problem. Sometimes we had to travel abroad for work. Once you get hooked on a Siamese it becomes very hard to go away and leave them. They seem to know this and are very good at making you feel guilty; staring through the window with sorrowful eyes as you drive away and then getting straight on the phone to *Catline*, the feline version of Esther Rantzen's child protection charity.

But, despite the guilt and regrets, in 1994 we hardened our hearts and embarked on a very long trip by car to Austria. I was speaking at a conference in Graz, but then fancied going on to Croatia to a place I had visited 10 years earlier called Umag. Looking back visiting the former Yugoslavia, while the civil war was still underway, was rather daring and arguably foolish. But youth tends not to see the risks and by this time the worst fighting was further south in Bosnia. When we got to Croatia it was sad to see the effect the war had exerted, although the Adriatic, with its crystal water and myriad of small islands, looked as wonderful as ever and it was clear that Croatia would recover. The real tragedy lay elsewhere.

So off we went in July 1994 on our three week long trip and Lucky had to go to a cattery up in the Neath valley; about a 20 mile drive away from where we lived. Lucky howled like a banshee all the way to the cattery, putting Benita's nerves on edge and leaving her a jabbering wreck at the end of the journey. The Siamese call, when it is distressed, is an incredibly disquieting sound. In fact it

18

makes a baby's cry sound like a church choir. When we got to the cattery the owner clearly saw our distress as quite comical and could not keep a straight face. We said that we would call every day to see how the little fellow was doing. He though this most amusing and on reflection I can see now that he just thought we were potty. We drove away with Lucky staring at us like someone who had been handed over to the Welsh branch of Al Qaeda.

We got back from our 3000 mile drive in one piece and our adventures in Croatia and Austria passed without generating either drama or danger. Our two most remarkable experiences concerned a barking mad Bavarian hotelier, who kept screaming at me 'Haben Sie ein wunsch', and a predatory Canadian academic who kept trying to put his hand up Benita's skirt. This person warranted the proverbial "bunch of fives". But Benita, ever the diplomat, only recounted Lothario's overtures when we were safely in Croatia. Overall we handled these two episodes with aplomb and were soon back safe and sound in South Wales.

Being back home there was only one urgent issue and that was being re-united with our forsaken Siamese. After we had rapidly unpacked we motored off up to the Neath valley to get our beloved feline back. And guess what? He was in one piece and looked fine. The cattery owner was still smirking and clearly amazed that we really had called from all over Europe to check on Lucky's welfare. He repeated the howling banshee routine all the way back to Sketty, I am sure Doreen Tovey would have said that he was telling us what rotters we were and how we had been gone for an eternity. Whatever "Luxie" was saying it left us riddled with guilt and regrets. We vowed that he was not going into a cattery again and during our next trip abroad a woman friend from the University came in to see to his needs at home. But letting people come into your house unsupervised is always a risk. As it turned out my female friend was conducting a passionate affair with one of my senior colleagues; someone I viscerally disliked. She and he needed a maison d'amour for some covert liaisons. But "Dick Dastardly", as I called him, was not someone who was welcome at Chez Lawrence and I was deeply

19

unhappy to eventually discover that he had had access to our house and Lucky. He was no cat lover. Fortunately this problem is no more, as today in Somerset, we have people that we can really trust who look after our current Siamese tribe.

Daft as a brush

In her books Doreen Tovey made great play of the fact that the cats were sending her and Charles bonkers. Maybe this was a slight exaggeration for artistic effect, but pets, and cats in particular, certainly have a way of making you look daft. The Toveys found themselves in many embarrassing situations triggered by Siamese antics. I can empathise. One day I was in our back garden trying to photograph our little chap for posterity. Bear in mind this was with old style celluloid film, not today's digital technology. Nowadays you can shoot hundreds of exposures in the hope that some are decent and the cost is minimal. But not so then, developing and printing was expensive and nobody wanted a camera full of duff pictures. So I was trying to get it right.

My subject was not playing ball. He was sunning himself on some steps at the back of the garden that led up to a garage. I was at the bottom of the steps waving and cooing and trying to get him to stare at the camera. I am sure readers have experienced that infuriating thing cats do to photographers, which is to look away just as you click the shutter. So I was waving, jumping up and down, making daft noises and generally behaving like a complete mental case. I don't know what instinct guided me at that particular moment, but I had a sense that someone was watching me and I turned around. Sure enough, my neighbour, who was also a lecturer at the university, was staring through his bedroom window at my bizarre antics. I felt such a fool, made worse by the fact that Chris was a very serious and upright individual, indeed, one destined to become the Vice Chancellor of a leading UK University. I just smiled wanly and wished the earth would open and swallow me up. I ended the photography session and went indoors.

The business with the cattery had made us very nervy about transporting Lucky in the car. But soon a much longer journey was in the offing, as I had been offered a new academic job in Bristol, where my beloved also worked. I felt very bad that she had to do so much travelling and I had been seeking a position back in the South West of England for some time. Now I had succeeded and we were soon to be on the move again, with a two hour car journey in the offing, accompanied by the cat who howled like a klaxon horn from Hades. I said that I would wear ear plugs and take him on my own!

With a certain inevitability, on the night before our move to South Gloucestershire in 1995, Lucky would not come back into the house. Benita, now my wife, had predicted this outcome and was beside herself with anxiety. I assured her that it would all be ok, but at one o'clock with no sign of Lucky, I too was getting worried. But then I had an idea. It was a long shot, but I recalled that whenever I sat in the garden or lay on the grass to do a spot of sun bathing, Lucky would come and sit on my chest or stomach, just to make sure that I was warm enough! So I thought that if I went out to do a bit of moon bathing, Lucky might come to investigate and I could grab him. I also thought that as we had an infra-red security light at the rear of the house he was sure to be able to see me. So I gave it a try and at 1:15am I went into the back garden and lay supine on the rear lawn in the full glow of our 300 watt spotlight, hoping that the missing moggie would turn up.

After ten minutes or so there was no sign of our errant night owl so I began to call his name. But it was to no avail. However, I had aroused the same neighbour who had seen me doing my photography routine and now he and his very proper German wife were staring at me from their rear bedroom window. So for the second time in a few months, in the grand tradition of Doreen Tovey, a daft behaviour triggered by (in this case) a *half* Siamese cat had convinced onlookers that I was bonkers. I think Chris and his wife were just glad that the lunatic next door was moving away. It was like one of those scenes in the BBC comedy series, *One Foot in the Grave,* when Patrick spots Victor Meldrew doing something crazy next door. However, in this case I didn't really care; I was on a mission to find that darn cat! In the end my eccentric strategy did pay off and Lucky appeared, seemingly curious to investigate the lunatic lying on the lawn at 2am in the morning. I grabbed him without ceremony and marched into the house. My beloved wife was eternally grateful and accorded me knight in shining armour status. As most men will know this kind of hero worship is always short-lived. But I played it for all it was worth at the time.

3

Off to Gloucestershire

On a gorgeous sunny day in July 1995 we departed for our new life in South Gloucestershire in two cars, with the removal truck bringing up the rear. As I had promised, I took Lucky with me to spare my wife the excruciating wailing noise that accompanied me all the way to North Bristol. As is always the case with house moves our transition to Bristol was not without its little frustrations.

The wrong arm of the law

When we arrived at our new property at about 2pm the local agents refused to give us the keys. This was because our solicitor in Swansea had not actually transferred the money to the vendor's legal team. So there we were, sitting on a suburban road in south Gloucestershire, with our two cars, a Siamese cat and a truck and three removal men. This time I had not used our cat hating solicitor friend with the water pistol, but someone from one of Swansea's biggest firms.

I have to say, that based on a number of disastrous experiences, I am not a huge fan of the legal profession in general. After waiting about 30 minutes for the keys without result, I called *Badger, Fox and Badger* at their Swansea office. Back in those days mobile phones were a fairly rare and novel item, but I had just acquired a Motorola. It was about the size of a house brick and the battery only lasted 30 minutes, but sometimes it did work. Today I was in luck and I got through to the legal eagle's secretary back in South Wales. I soon discovered that our conveyancer, Rod Jenkins, was at lunch at a hostelry on the Walter Road in Swansea. Apparently there had not been time to do a CHAPS bank transfer before lunch. So I enquired as to when this gentlemen might return from his repast? I was informed that lunch on a Friday could go on 'quite some time'!

This was a troubling prospect, but I had a fairly good idea where Mr Jenkins was taking luncheon, so I had the temerity to call the pub and tell the landlord that I needed "Rod the law" on the phone tout suite, as it was an emergency. Eventually, a very disgruntled Mr. Jenkins came to the phone and gave me a real chewing over for interrupting his libations. To be candid we had a heck of a row and I must confess that I conveyed some colourful descriptions, both of him and his profession. Even the removal men, one of whom was a bit of an intellectual and a Physics Ph.D no less, looked shocked by my language.

With regard to my acute annoyance perhaps I should add that not long before we had discovered that an endowment mortgage that Benita had taken out on another property in Bristol did not actually have the endowment set up. That particular cock-up was down to our water pistol toting anti-Siamese legal friend and a bunch of idiots at a now defunct building society. Anyway, my row with Dai the lunch culminated in him slamming the receiver down. Lucky was howling away in his cage, Benita was sobbing and the removal men looked glum. Curtains in the close were also twitching. We eventually got our keys at around 3:30pm. I will never know if my intervention accelerated the process or slowed it down.

Lucky settles in

Although I had sworn on oath that Lucky would not stay in a cattery again, I must confess that on this first night in North Bristol, Lucky was traduced and taken to a cattery at Filton, while we put our new house in order. We were very fortunate that Benita had two great pals from work who helped us get sorted. They were also mad animal lovers like us. Indeed, Sara was the daughter of a vet from

Jersey who had been a close friend of Gerald Durrell, no less. With Nick and Sara's help we were "ship shape and Bristol fashion" in no time and the trauma of being locked out was forgotten. The next day we fetched Lucky back to the small village near Chipping Sodbury, where we had bought the new house. I just hoped that not too many people in Church Close had heard me cursing on the telephone.

We were very smitten with our new abode, which was slightly larger than our Swansea house and also a detached property, with a bigger garden and blessedly safe from traffic. Even better, neighbours could not see into our garden. So now my daft antics would not be so visible. Lucky soon settled in and after us "lurpaking" his paws again he was allowed out to explore. In those days we were not so paranoid about cat safety and he roamed freely, as his fancy dictated. There was plenty of open green space outside and he seemed in his element and went on to spend a relatively tranquil three years in South Gloucestershire.

The only bugbear was an extremely aggressive, big and crafty tabby tom cat who lived next door and gave Lucky a hard time. He was a very big cat and a real bully. I tried to discuss the situation with said tom on a number of occasions, but he was too fast and crafty for me. Still, his charming owner looked after Lucky when Benita and I were away, which was very kind and very fortunate for us. She also had two charming and very pretty daughters, who were in their late 20s. They were always inviting me around for tea and, as I told Benita, I felt that a refusal would have been ungracious.

I was happy to be back in South West England and excited by the prospect of my new job. The only drawback for me on leaving Swansea was that it made it somewhat more complicated for me to see my two sons, who still lived over in Wales. But in fact they spent most of the school summer holidays of 95 with us and came to live in Bristol not long after. They were worried about losing Lucky, as they were very fond of him. This was largely a mutual affection, although cats do not like boisterous kids. Indeed, they will not mix easily with kids at all unless they have encountered them as young kittens. However, Lucky was fine with children and, as it turned out, my boys saw plenty of him during that long hot summer. Siamese have a certain reputation for being difficult, but this has not been the case with the ones that have blessed our household. Lucky never scratched, bit or put a paw wrong in any respect. He was a real gent.

Lucky enjoyed himself enormously at the new house and had discovered many interesting fauna to play with in the garden, including a colony of frogs. There was a small village green in front of our house with a stream and pond. I assumed that the frogs were plentiful because of the proximity of water. We would be in the house and hear this frightful shrieking sound, which was a frog crying while being bashed by Lucky, who liked batting their heads with his paws. Clearly, the claws were extended thus causing the shrieks, but Lucky never actually killed the frogs and never bit them. He just liked whacking them on the head. The other regular visitors we had that summer were hedgehogs, who often seemed de-hydrated because of the heat. Many a bucket of water was taken out to relieve tired and thirsty hedgehogs. Lucky gave them a wide birth as, by and large, felines are very skilled at knowing what is not suitable prey. Lucky killed very few small mammals and his behaviour re-enforced my long held belief that well fed domestic cats are not often great hunters.

Lucky's biggest problem was the tom next door who was the neighbourhood thug. One of the fights with Tom (the tom was called Tom) required a vet's visit for a small operation and some stitches. Unfortunately, it's just a fact of life that some Toms, especially un-neutered ones, will dominate and bully other cats. In some cases entering other cat's houses and stealing food. One night Tom did in fact get in through our cat flap and there was a hell of a scene as we tried to guide him back outside. As we witnessed, a terrified and angry tom cat can be quite a challenge to handle, even when you are trying to help him. By the time of his departure our kitchen looked like a tornado had hit, with overturned chairs and broken crockery everywhere, not to mention a dead toaster lying upside down on the floor. I must admit we were glad to finally get the little desperado (another term was used at the time) out of the door.

Lucky's other problem concerned our neighbours on the opposite side from Tom, who were strange. They used to throw buckets of water on him. They were rather weird folks who would not answer the door to any visitors. But they can't have been all bad as they owned a pretty little tabby that Lucky had taken a shine to. It often surprises owners, and in my experience even vets, but neutered cats do retain an interest in matters of the heart, or more accurately the loins. So yes, I have to admit that Lucky had the "hots" for the little cutey next door and our strange neighbours did not like it. One evening we were outside on the green at the front of our house when Lucky came charging towards us howling like an Apache on the warpath. As he got closer we realised that he was soaking wet. Our neighbours were not far behind, but came to an abrupt halt when they saw our looming presence. The woman, to whom we had never really spoken, blurted out, "you think we have thrown water on your cat, but we didn't". I, lying through my teeth, muttered that "we thought no such thing", upon which the dowsers of amorous cats turned on their heels and went home.

We never saw them again to speak to, except for one occasion when I had foolishly taken in a parcel, which the postman had asked me to pass on when they returned. This turned out to be a big mistake, as I found myself repeatedly walking around to their house, knocking the door or ringing the bell and getting no reply, even when I could see them through the window. After about a month or so of this stupidity I eventually lost my cool and just yelled through their window that "I would like them to open the bloody door as I had a package for them". Sheepishly they came to the door and took the package and we never spoke again. In some ways it was a strange old place our village in South Gloucestershire. Being an avuncular northerner, I am used to people being fairly open and direct. But our local village neighbours were rather privatised and suspicious of people that were too direct. A real, full on Yorkshire man would have frightened them to death. Still, as the Germans say, *"Andere länder, andere sitten"*.

Football support

At certain periods in their history domestic cats have been thought to have mystical powers. The ancient Egyptians worshipped them as Gods and even had a bizarre cult of cat sacrifice, at the same time as forbidding that cats be harmed on pain of death. The Egyptian attitude was contradictory, with cats bred specifically for slaughter as well as being venerated. But there was nothing contradictory about the attitude of Christianity to cats in the Middle Ages in Western Europe. Cats were associated with witchcraft and paganism and persecuted to near extinction in some areas; they were believed to have dark and magical powers. Many tens of thousands were burned alive, and in towns such as Ypres, in Belgium, cats were flung to their death from the clock tower. They were lovely people, these late medieval Christians.

I also believe that cats have special powers, but I admire this and I don't see them as Satan's little pal. So I confess that I used to ask Lucky for some magical help with little problems, like my football team for instance. Being a West Ham United supporter is a curse that I inherited from my Dad. He enjoyed the glory years of Bobby Moore, Geoff Hurst and Martin Peters. You may remember that West Ham, more or less on their own, won the World Cup for England back in 1966. But I have had the constant battle against relegation, the spells back in the 2nd division (now the Championship) and of course, the West Ham Utd special. This is to be two or even three nil ahead in a key game and then lose. Remember the 2006 FA Cup Final, as soon as the second goal went in for West Ham I knew it was hopeless. Late in the second half the TV commentator announced that Liverpool's Steven Gerrard looked "dead on his feet" and would surely be "substituted any second". About a minute later Gerrard struck a 30 yards thunderbolt into the back of the West Ham net. Liverpool had levelled at 3:3. I didn't even watch the penalty shoot out.

As the results suggest the Lucky magic did not always work, even Gandalf and Bilbo Baggins would struggle with West Ham. But despite the long odds, I would ask Lucky to weave a spell and urge an improbable victory in key games. I remember an FA Cup game against Blackburn Rovers in 1997, when the replay ended as a draw at Ewood Park. West Ham won the penalty shoot out. That was a miracle in itself and I was convinced that my feline companion had put in a good word. Of course really I know it's all nonsense, but when you are stuck with a team like West Ham you will try anything. Recent events have increased both my desperation and humiliation. My beloved team have just managed to exit the League and FA Cup in consecutive games where the aggregate score was 0:11. Benita thinks that I should switch to a decent team, but I couldn't do it. Only a man would understand.

On the road again

Life in our South Gloucestershire village was good, but it was a 15 mile commute into the North of Bristol, where we both worked. Also, although our house was pleasant, there was nothing special or compelling about the area. So, much to my beloved's frustration, I began to get itchy feet again. Maybe I have some gypsy blood, as I felt certain that it was time for another move. Also Lucky was fed up with being bullied by Big Tom next door and was doing a bit of crafty spraying under the stairs. This is typical behaviour of a cat that is stressed. We had to up sticks.

I had discovered a little development in a village just on the fringe of North Bristol, that I thought was idyllic. From there it was only one mile for me and two miles for Benita to work. A house came up at in just the right place and at the right price so we were off again. The vendor's were cat people and the house was cat friendly. We were to meet these lovely people, who sold us the house, again 11 years later in rather odd circumstances. But more of than anon.

This time we were "on a roll", as they say in the US. Even the solicitor was satisfactory. Lucky had to be uprooted again, but as I explained to him he would escape the local bully and also his unwanted dowsing from the mad neighbours. As a result, in December 1998, after just three years, we left South Gloucestershire to move to a lovely part of Bristol, called Frenchay. Frenchay, part village and part suburb, was a great environment for a gentleman cat. There was not too much traffic back then and lots of interesting greenery and a wood and river bank to explore. The three of us set off for our new life with great excitement. I even thought we might settle in the new place permanently, but as we shall see, this was not to be. Although Lucky did spend the rest of his days in Frenchay. Benita, now completely fed up with moving home, did at least get a decade of respite at the new property. It was the longest that we have ever stayed at any house.

4

Lucky in Bristol

Lucky spent 10 idyllic years in Bristol. He was master of a big house and lived in a quiet suburban avenue. He even had a charming tabby lady friend next door. We were often away abroad for work reasons, but a charming family called the Browns went in to look after him. Opposite our house was a huge detached property where two doctors lived. This house had a large front garden with a pool stocked with fish. In the summer Lucky would saunter, (agonisingly slowly) across the road and into Dr Tom's garden. Tom and his wife had no pets, so Lucky had free range on their property. Nothing was ever said, but we were sure that Lucky occasionally availed himself of a nice goldfish or two. All things considered our doctor friends were very reasonable about the whole thing, only remarking a couple of times that they were always restocking the pond. We told them, without trying to look guilty, that the herons, which were nearby on the river Frome, were known to take fish.

Lucky, now living up to his moniker, got on famously in Frenchay and established a good rapport with a feline lady friend next door, who was a charming little tabby, called Dolly. This time our neighbours (Alan and Janet) were both rational and utterly charming, as well as cat lovers. Nor did they want to impose Sharia law on the cats. Lucky and Dolly were even permitted to have a little love nest in the shape of a garden shed complete with cat flap for access and blankets during cold weather.

Lucky, having given up on any titbits coming down from the table above.

So this was catopia. Our little cross-Siamese had the life of Riley. Lucky didn't even have to go by car to the vets, as my adoring wife had decided this was too stressful, mainly for her. So the vet came to us on house visits. I often pondered the fact that GPs would no longer come to the house, but that the vet does. Benita says that they also give better care. Of course we never mentioned this to Tom, our GP friend across the road.

It was great to have smashing neighbours and no anti-cat types in the neighbourhood. Our good friends on the other side to Dolly, were not really animal lovers, but they were just neutral, not hostile. Just down from Tom across the road lived a charming elderly lady called Janice, who owned a lovely little terrier, who she called Honey. Janice, who was a real sweetie, used to amuse us as, although in her 80s, she still spoke of the days back when "Mummy and Daddy" were alive. She adored Lucky and would come and visit regularly. Although not with Honey. Generally, it was all idyllic. But of course you always have one nutcase. The other side of Janet and

Alan lived an elderly brother and sister. The lady was fine, but the chap was bonkers, even without the impact of a Siamese in the house. In those days I owned a large, black Mercedes saloon. When I drove past, this gentleman would stand to attention and do the NAZI salute. I never knew if it was admiration, or contempt. Perhaps he had never got over the war.

A friend in need

Nothing lasts forever, as they say, and after four or five tranquil years in 2006 a great shadow loomed large in our house as it was discovered that I had that terrible disease, the one John Wayne had called the "Big C". I had thought something was wrong for some time, but in typical male fashion had ignored the symptoms. The problem was then spotted during a routine examination and I owed a debt to an observant young locum at our practice who saw something he didn't like the look of and, in no time, a consultant surgeon at a local hospital had rammed a syringe into my chest, taken a biopsy and told me bluntly, when the results came back, that I had grade three, stage two cancer. This was on a Tuesday. I was shell-shocked and walked out of the hospital like a zombie. On the Friday of the same week I had a CT scan that was analysed on the spot and it was ascertained that the cancer had not spread beyond the original site. I had a reasonable chance of a cure. The scan result meant that I might well live! Then something slightly surreal happened.

In those days I did the occasional TV news interview, as I was the local "expert" on the aircraft industry; which is a big and prestigious employer in Bristol. While waiting for the CT scan result with Benita I had a call from ITV news who asked me to go down to the studio to do the lunchtime bulletin. Mainly because it was a diversion from the stressful business of waiting for the scan result, I agreed to go down to the Bath road studios in Bristol and do an interview.

En route to the studio my consultant called me with good news about the scan. When I walked into the studio the presenter, who I knew slightly, saw me and remarked, "Hiya, you look cheerful, had some good news"? Quick as a flash I replied, "Yeah, I've just heard that I am not going to die". He looked at Benita, who was with me, and replied, "Bloody hell, he's a bit of a card, isn't he". So I just pretended it was a joke. But you know the old adage: if you want to fool people tell them the truth.

Back in the real world I had 8 months of exhausting treatment to endure; including surgery, chemotherapy and radiotherapy. After it was over, I just had to rest and recover. "Chemo" puts highly toxic "free radicals" into the body and they make you feel awful. But throughout my rehabilitation I had a constant companion (two in fact) who looked after me. My carer during the day was, of course, Lucky, who was a great and constant source of comfort. I spent the wet summer of 2007 dozing on the sofa and ploughing through the Ian Rankin, Rebus books. Lucky was by my side, purring away the whole time. If you are trying to recover from a trauma or illness you can't beat a friendly pet for boosting your spirits and your optimism. I have no idea if he knew how much he was helping me, but he did a great job. Sadly, though, I feel out of love with the Rankin books as I realised that D. I. Rebus was a bit of a cat hater. In one book he and a colleague discover a dead cat in a freezer. He wittily exclaims, "cool for cats". I gave all the books to the cat's protection charity shop in revenge.

In a rather vicious twist of fate, just as I was really feeling better, Benita and I got some very bad news about our feline friend and companion. In the winter of 2007 it was discovered that Lucky had cancer of the larynx. Siamese make some very strange noises, but his voice had become faint and hoarse and he was losing weight. After diagnosis euthanasia was recommended, but we demurred and had his cancer treated with chemotherapy, which initially seemed quite successful. As the treatment, which was done down in Bridgewater, proceeded we became quite optimistic that his life might be extended for a significant time.

As if this were not enough of a bad turn, in the middle of the treatment Lucky also had a terrible experience, when he was shot by some maniac with an airgun. It was around Christmas time in 2007 and he disappeared into his room and went to ground for two days. We checked on him, but thought that he was just feeling low because of the treatment. Eventually, we took him to the vet, who discovered that he had been shot. Fortunately, the pellet had hit a rib and bounced out again. But there was clear evidence of a puncture wound and the vet, who had seen the same thing many times, was sure it was caused by an airgun. Of course we felt very guilty and were mortified that we had not examined him more thoroughly. And these episodes are doubly horrible, first, because of the act of cruelty against the pet and secondly, because you become suspicious of people in the vicinity and generally it makes you feel very misanthropic. We discovered that some local scouts had an airgun shooting range down by the river Frome and it was difficult not to picture one of them as the culprits. But there was no evidence and, despite their popularity as pets, cats have many enemies. We wrote an article for the village magazine warning cat owners about the risk and we crossed our fingers in hope that it was a one-off event.

Generally cats arouse strong emotions and we knew that there were some cat haters in the neighbourhood. If one wanted to "vent some spleen", as they say, one could add that the kind of people who advocate cat control and sometimes culling, because of the toll they take on small mammals and birds are unhelpful in this context. Contrary to what is often argued, the figures given out publicly for the loss of wildlife due to cats are largely guesswork. A recent *Horizon* programme on the BBC indicated that cat hunting is much less successful than has been thought and that the predatory toll is rather lower than previously believed. Having said that, Benita and I believe that responsible owners should keep cats inside at night, which is safer for them and their potential prey. But some folks just hate cats for the sake of it.

Lucky towards the end of his life and after the shooting incident.
He was very poorly and needed a good deal of medical support.

As has already been mentioned the Medieval church in Europe associated cats with paganism and persecuted them remorselessly from the 14th century. There was even a papal edict compelling anyone who saw a black cat after dark to kill or maim the poor victims of this lunacy. Such was the gentle and forgiving character of Medieval christianity. Cats have also had some famous enemies; Alexander the Great, Napoleon and Hitler all hated cats. But some good guys stand on the other side; including Winston Churchill, Leonardo da Vinci and Ernest Hemingway. So, we knew what we were looking for in trying to find Lucky's evil assailant; we were either seeking a small man with a world domination complex, or maybe some mad cleric who was stalking Frenchay with an airgun. We never found out, which was probably better for both the perpetrator and us.

Lucky gradually recovered from the trauma of being shot and, even with the cancer treatment, his quality of life in the Spring of

2008 was fairly good. Felines really are resilient creatures and he handled the chemotherapy, with the drug vincristine, very well. But in May 2008, on a horrible wet Sunday, he deteriorated very fast and died. We wrapped him in one of Benita's old dressing gowns that he had liked to lie on and put him in a wooden Chateau Margaux wine box with some of his favourite toys. He was buried with due ceremony in the back garden, where he still rests close to his beloved Dolly, who passed on this year. I wrote a poem to express our sense of grief at the time.

5

Siamese Arrival

We had been thinking about finding a new Siamese kitten to keep Lucky company towards the end of his life, but his rapid deterioration made that impossible. However, I had seen a little fellow on a breeder's web site that had caught my eye. In fact he was a black oriental short hair, by the unlikely name of Stringfellow Cwmkatz. The oriental short hair is a breed created in the 1950s from Siamese stock and they are all but indistinguishable from their Thai cousins, except for their colour. The Orientals' coat is normally a "solid" colour, like black, cinnamon or light brown (the Havana) etc. They also should have green, emerald-coloured eyes. The males, in particular, tend to be bigger than normal Siamese and they are even more noisy. They bond with humans very strongly and tend to have one individual who is the special person in their lives.

The advert for Stringfellow was compelling as it spoke of him "desperately seeking his forever home". Being a sucker for a hard luck story I didn't realise that this was standard breeder talk in sales' adverts. But in fact this little chap had been "bought" twice and on both occasions the potential new owners had pulled out. Benita was not really ready for a new kitten and felt a sense of mild betrayal to Lucky. But I felt the need to fill the void and move on, so I convinced myself that this little mite needing rescuing. As a result, not long after Lucky's passing, off we went down the M5 motorway to Paington, on the South Devon coast.

As Dr. McCoy might have said in Star Trek: "It's a cat Phil, but not as we have ever known one" Leo trying (and succeeding) to look like ET.

We soon tracked Stringfellow down and were sitting in his owner's living room surrounded by four or five dogs and cats. But "String", as his breeder Glynis called him, was hiding in a pen in the corner of the living room. I had never seen an oriental short hair cat close up before and it was an amazing sight. Their most arresting feature is their huge ears that stick out like a pair of delta wings on an aircraft. So the overall ensemble is a sleek and svelte body, with high gloss coat and the classic modern Siamese triangular head, topped with enormous ears. String, or Leo as we soon came to call him, looked like a cross between ET and Dobby, the elf from the Harry Potter films. Back then he was truly one of the most extraordinary cats that I had ever seen. I call his ears "Jodrells", after the Jodrell Bank space telescope in Cheshire.

However, it was also clear that Leo was very shy and nervous. Most behavioural experts would have advised a potential owner to walk away. He was getting on for 6 months and not really a kitten anymore. But as I had convinced myself that we were there on a rescue mission, leaving him behind was out of the question. The breeder actually seemed very surprised that we wanted him and even mentioned that he had a bit of a "gippy" tummy and was having organic yoghurt added to his food! But we were already smitten with old big ears and within a few minutes Leo was in our cat box and deposited on the back seat of our car, ready for the journey back to Bristol.

As readers will know Siamese and Orientals are notorious for both the type and amount of noise they make. But in this case the cat with ears like bat wings (Doreen Tovey used to call her first male Siamese "old bat ears") stayed mute all the way back to Bristol, presumably convinced that he had been subject to some form of extraordinary rendition. When we arrived in Frenchay we let him out of the cat box in the hallway and he disappeared behind a large sofa in the small sitting room.

Leo remained behind the sofa for three weeks. By the end of week one I wondered what on earth we had done. It was lovely having a new cat, but seeing him once in a while would have been nice too. But no! We had acquired a cat more reclusive than Howard Hughes or Stanley Kubrick. Only food bowls in the kitchen, that we found to be empty in the morning, were proof that the black shadow was really there.

We also soon realised he was smart. We were giving him top notch grub from posh looking sachets. And Leo proved that he didn't need our help to get into the cupboard and find his special packets of food. He could also open the sachets without our assistance. In addition, during his first few days with us, he helped himself to half a sliced loaf of white bread, which was regurgitated on the kitchen floor. And yes, this is another endearing habit of the Siamese; eating the wrong stuff at breakneck speed and then bringing it up tout suite. Leo might be shy, but with his own sneaky brand of self service, he certainly wasn't going to go short of food. But more important for us at that time was the question:

How could we get Leo (aka the thief of Baghdad) to appear and actually join our household in a visible way? **The answer: cherchez la femme!**

Coco Chanel: a posh lady from Surrey

I have to confess that my favourite Siamese is the seal point. Doreen Tovey was right that there is something utterly compelling about the black mask ,with the piercing sapphire blue eyes. And of course the luxurious mink, cream and caramel coloured fur. So, as a match and pal for Leo, we decided to find a female seal point kitten. At this time we were not really aware of the key differences between the modern Siamese and the so called traditionals. So that was not a significant criterion for us. We just wanted a seal point. We contacted a breeder over in Milton Keynes, whose web site we had seen, but she had no kittens due. However, one of this lady's friends had recently mated her queen with one of the breeder's very handsome looking toms, called Bubic.

Coco's German father, Bubic, looking very pleased with himself,
as well he might!

And, we were in luck, this lady had kittens to sell! But they were the more rounded looking traditional Siamese and not the more fashionable moderns. Also Bubic was German so we knew that any kittens would be even more self confident and bossy than normal. In fact the idea of a German Siamese was slightly mind boggling. But we didn't let any of this dampen our enthusiasm and we soon made contact and before long we were motoring along the M4 motorway over to Wokingham in Surrey to view a litter of gorgeous seal points, with a German sounding meow.

We selected Coco Chanel, as her breeder had called her, and returned about four weeks later to pick her up and take her back to Bristol to meet her retiscent partner Leo, or Mr Leezey, as he is also known. Unlike Leo, Coco screetched and squawked on the journey back down the M4 in typical Siamese fashion and we felt that we had got the genuine article. She arrived and settled into life in Frenchay very quickly. Although not without perfuming our bed on her first morning in Frenchay, with a bit of cat scent, just to announce her presence.

But, despite Coco's arrival and Benita's attempts to coax him out with chicken tidbits, there was still no sign of Leo and we let a few days pass before an attempt was made to introduce our two new Siamese children. Then we took Coco into the small sitting room, which was Leo's secret bunker, and waited to see what would happen. Eventually, after a couple of false starts, a small, black, string-like creature appeared from behind the sofa and approached Ms. Chanel. Coco promptly hissed, barred her teeth and spat at the faint hearted Romeo, who disappeared quick as a flash. Such is the downside of a blind date for cats. A few days later another encounter ensued in a bedroom and the sounds of aggression were more muted. Then a third meeting resulted in sniffs, murmurs and eventually some mutual grooming. Friendship had been established. Fairly soon afterwards the two new pals became inseperable and were romping around the house wreaking havoc. Two Siamese was definitely much more than double the fun, but it was of course also double trouble.

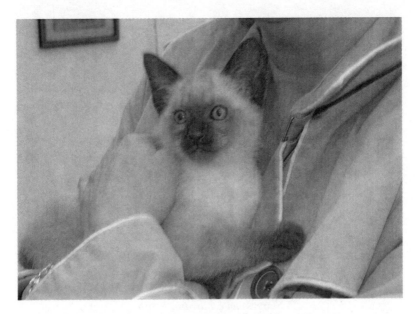

*Coco at 7 weeks. Trying the new Mum out for size! She has remained
the most affectionate and balanced of cats. Not like the two "moderns"
who are bonkers.*

Coco was a gorgeous kitten; very gregarious and amusing with a
penchant for hiding in wine boxes or the kind of handled straw
baskets that people put ornamental flowers in. She and Leo were
clearly very happy and her confidence seemed to make him come
out of his shell and behave a little more normally. Although he would
still run away if either of us walked too fast in his direction, or if a
stranger came into the house. It was amazing where he could hide.
He could flatten all four legs on the floor, looking like a cat-shaped
star fish, and slide under very low pieces of furniture, such as a HiFi
unit or chest of drawers. I already mentioned that he looked a bit like
ET and this performance was like something out of the X Files.

The ability to hide under furniture also caused us some anxiety.
Sometimes Leo would disappear and we would be certain that he
had escaped and gone AWOL. But then, miraculously, he would re-
appear, as if by majic. On many an occasion we never worked out
where Houdini had been hiding.

Coco and Leo just recovering after a late night.
Siamese love to lie in the sun.

As time passed Leo's reticence was just something we came to accept, but events like taking him to the vet for check ups or jabs were a nightmare. On one occasion we were trying to get him into a catbox to get him to the vet. After several hours of playing silly sods I eventually got him cornered on the landing, with seemingly no way past me. Or so I thought, until to my utter amazement, he climbed vertically up the wall and did a wall of death routine running horizontally past me along the wall, like the character **Trinity** in one of the opening seens of the film *The Matrix*. It was actually quite a scary experience, as it illustrated just how powerful Leo was. The oriental shorthair is a cat comprised almost entirely of muscle. By this time he was about 4.5 kilos in weight and clearly able to pull off the most extraordinary physical stunts.

He performed the same wall of death routine one day when our younger son was trying to pick him up and Alex was also shaken and awed by the experience. Eventually we became reconciled to the fact that the only person who could coax him into any direct contact was Benita. She had also discovered the great gastronomic love of his life, which is roast chicken. If a freshly cooked drumstick was available we found Leo much more pliable. Although the fare had to be basted with butter and lighly dusted with paprika. But this discovery had a downside. When Leo Stringfellow wants some chicken the racket that he creates would awaken the dead. This is a cat that knows his culinary rights and has a built in foghorn available for protest marches and sit-ins when chicken is not available. It is not a pretty sound.

Leo the great ninja enjoying the sun after a bit of chicken satay. Not a cat you want to cross, if you know what's good for you!

The mating game

Before going the whole hog and acquiring two pedigree Siamese we had done some homework and knew a liitle of what we had let ourselves in for. We were aware, for example, that when a Siamese female (queen) comes into season her call can be pretty disquieting. However, nothing really prepares you for the actual experience. Coco came into season for the first time just after we had got past the trauma of Guy Fawkes night in Novermber 2008. She and Leo slept in a room acoss the landing from our bedroom. But during the firework season they would get frightened and howl outside our room to be let in. But then Ms. Chanel started making some noise of her own.

Coco started quite slowly with about 30 minutes calling on the first night. But this was just an overture. The Wagner had not yet begun. From then on, night and day, the most earsplitting racket was emitted by our little Juliet. Calling for a mate, or seeking a husband as Doreen Tovey used to say of her cats, is a serious business. The noise is really alarming. When I was a child a little girl who lived further along in our road was once stung by a bee. She shrieked and cried so loudly you cold hear the noise 200 yards away. This was the same kind of noise, with the same kind of penetration, yet more disturbing. And it's not just the noise, the poor little mite started behaving like a sex mad lunatic. She would crawl along the floor on her tummy with her bottom raised in the air and rub scent furiously on furniture doors and your legs if you happened to be about. It is clearly a process that takes complete control of a female cat.

The noise and weird behaviour was taxing, to say the least. However, in addition we had a steady parade of motley local toms who came to our doors and windows to check on the action and the lady's availability. The bushes close to our front door began to pong of cat pee; quite embarrassing when visitors called. I think I can honestly say that of all the behaviours one has to cope with from a Siamese, this was the most exacting. We had been debating whether to let Coco have a litter of kittens, but this calling episode gave us our clear answer. It lasted about 10 days and it was a huge relief when it was over. A full night's sleep had not been possible during the whole episode. The only sound that I had ever heard that was worse was from a female Lynx that I had seen in a zoo near Plymouth some years before. The sound that she had made was so bad I went off to find a keeper, convinced that the poor animal was seriously ill and on her last legs. The keeper just laughed and explained that the lynx was in season.

Coco at about 4 months old. Siamese love to lie in warm sunlight. Coco was able to play cute and coquettish to a tee.

What was really worrying about this experience with Coco was that the first season was often shorter and less intense than subsequent periods of calling. In other words and quite unbelievably it could only get worse! So we promptly booked a spaying at the vets. I was a little guilty about this, as the female operation does carry some risk. Indeed, as I revealed in chapter one, Doreen Tovey's first Siamese female, Sugieh, had died during neutering surgery. But it had to be done! We opted for the procedure where the surgeon goes in through the flank, as this is quicker and less complex than spaying done via an incision into the tummy. Owners of pedigrees often opt for the latter, as when the fur returns on the site of the incision after an operation, it can sometimes be a slightly different colour; in a seal-point often darker. In fact this is exactly what happened with Coco, but all that mattered to us was that she was fine after the op and recovered quickly.

We need not have worried as Coco was charging about and acting as nothing had happened on the day that she came back from the surgery. She takes everything in her stride, provided plenty of grub is available. One thing that became very clear to us as we now had a "modern" and a "trad" Siamese is that the trads are much more balanced than the modern type. The modern's behaviour definitely matches their appearance. If you want the Siamese experience, but without the full spectrum of feline neurosis, the trad is the one to go for.

The Siamese steeplechase runners and riders at rest. Just getting ready for a quick 4 furlongs over the jumps around the house.

Antics

Doreen Tovey often talked of her cats sounding like they were taking part in a "steeplechase". Benita and I can identify with that observation very easily. The Siamese is a smart mover and Coco and Leo as youngsters would chase around the house at breakneck speed. What was extraordinary was that there would be no warning that one of these manic races was about to commence. One minute the Siamese desperados would be supine, dead to the world. The next they would be off like two rockets. The noise, if they were upstairs and we were listening downstairs, was quite incredible. On many an occasion visitors to our house would assume that adults or teenagers were moving around upstairs as the noise was so loud. What adults would be doing in our house running full tilt along corridors and in and out of rooms is another question.

One day a repair man was in our kitchen fixing our broken ceramic hob. Coco and Leo were doing a bit of training for the Cheltenham Gold Cup upstairs. I could see that he looked a little puzzled, if not concerned by the racket. So I volunteered an explanation, "Oh don't worry" I said, "that's just the cats charging about upstairs". Looking completely stunned he replied haltingly, "Uh, uhm.. what kind of cats are they". "Oh big cats" I replied, " we like big cats". The work was completed in record time and he was out of the house in a flash. I never clarified what I meant by "big cats" and I also realised that I might have a useful weapon in future, if any unwelcome visitors needed to be encouraged to leave. The cats didn't really like visitors anyway, especially if they stayed late and interupted meals or bed time.

The cacophany from the steeplechase was disturbing to visitors, although in a strange way we found it somehow comforting, as it seemed to be a powerful endorsement of the life-force. But, of course, not always pleasing when the odd vase or other valuable object got in the way. While the demonising image of Siamese in *Lady and the Tramp* is highly misleading, there is no doubt that they can be naughty and destructive, when the mood takes them. Benita calls Leo a "horiziontal scratcher". This is code for the fact that he likes to dig up the carpet, especially on the stairs. Coco is a vertical scratcher, which means she removes the wall paper. In Frenchay we had a yellow coloured paper that she really didn't like and it disappeared at a rate of knots. We don't paper walls anymore; just paint over the plaster in nice minimalist style. They don't bother about plaster and just leave it alone.

Coco the HiFi killer. She hates it when we go away and here she is making sure that I can't pack my trolley. She's just letting me know that I am "off my trolley".

Coco also seems to have it in for my stereo equipment, which is both valuable and very dear to my heart. At the Frenchay house I had two big column-style speakers in the main living room. They were about 3 feet high and 10 inches across. As all audiophiles know, such speakers normally have removable cloth/mesh grills on the front. Regrettably, to Coco, this type of speaker looks just like a scratching post. So the dear little mite (sometimes known as little Minx) would raise herself to her full height and sink her claws into the grill, just about where the tweeter (treble speaker cone) was in the cabinet. I would rush and remove said Siamese, only to find that cat and grill would come away together. Trying to get a 3ft speaker grill out of the claws of a Siamese is quite tricky. Coco would be standing on the floor, with the grill still stuck to her paws. She looked very odd, like a cat wearing giant snow shoes.

Thankfully this habit has now ceased. Siamese antics can just stop for no apparent reason. She probably thinks she has killed them. Fortunately, I found someone selling exactly the right grills for my speakers on ebay. A mere 10 quid sorted the problem. And yes, I put the new ones away until the habit had stopped. But the end of the stereo story is not entirely a happy one. Having got bored with my speakers, Coco has taken a shine to my Linn Sondek turntable; a piece of kit that middle-aged men, of a certain persuasion, drool over. She has now made two serious attempts on the life of this precious piece of audio treasure, one of which involved Mahler's fourth and is described below. I am hoping this habit ends soon.

At the time of writing the record deck is still alive and well, but sometimes the acts of destruction can be a bit much. At New Year 2008 we had gone away to a party in Lincolnshire. On the day we were driving back from Stamford our cat sitters called to say that there was quite a mess in the dining room. When we got back we found that a large and heavy gilt framed picture had been pulled off the wall and bounced off our mahogany sideboard, while simultaneously seeing off a large Waterford cristal vase, on its way to the floor. Miraculously, the mark on the sideboard was not too bad and the picture was salvaged. But the Waterford vase was in a thousand pieces. And of course our little beloveds greeted us with contrite stares suggesting implicitly that this was not their handywork. In fact we realised straight away that it was, of course, our fault and that we had made a tactical error with our Christmas decorations. Siamese love to tug on anything that is hanging down and we had put some decorative streamers around the tops of paintings and ornaments etc. So Coco, who we believe was the culprit, was just removing these foreign objects from the walls. "No harm meant", she appeared to tell us. Still one gives thanks for small mercies. The Toveys' cats had got inside and destroyed an antique grandfather clock. We could always find another Waterford vase. Though we never did!

In the meantime Leo's retexturing of the carpet and Coco's wall paper stripping continued. We were a bit fed up of the carpet in the main living room, as we had inherited some weird, psychadelic

Axminster from the charming couple who had sold us the house. We therefore decided that Coco and Leo simply didn't like the colour scheme and were nudging us towards a nicer looking replacment.

Sawasdee krahp: Thai food

Doubtless some readers will find this discomforting, but I have to confess that Coco and Leo tended to join us for dinner. Let me explain. Leo, as you have already heard, is very retiscent and my odd glimpse of old Flash was normally of him darting around the house at lightening speed from one safe haven to another. Over the years he has calmed down somewhat and now he is a respectable middle-aged gent he sits on the sofa next to Benita in the evening watching the TV. However, back in Frenchay, all I saw of him was a glossy black flashing object, hurtling around the house. Except when we were sat at the table having dinner. He would come into the dining room and just sit a couple of feet from the table watching amd assessing the grub. As time went by he started jumping onto the table and sat at the other end watching us eating. I hasten to add that he did not try and steal food off our plates. The dining table is quite large and he normally positioned hinself about 6 feet away from where we were sat. I decided that I did not mind as it was a good chance to actually see the little blighter. He only went a bit doolally if we were eating poultry and especially chicken. With apologies to non Goethe fans, I am sure that if Mephostophales turned up with a few drum sticks, Leo would be off like a shot to the gates of Hades with Dr. Faustus.

At first Coco did not join in our little supper parties as she is not remotely interested in human food. But then she too started to join us for the evening repast and Sunday lunch. Then something very strange happened and I am afraid this is going to sound hopelessly anthropomorphic; she started to sit on one of the dining chairs as though formally a diner at the meal. It looked very strange and prompted a bout of photography and the use of some corny captions. Coco has a way of staring directly at you with a rather formidable and determined stare, as though she is making some point in the strongest terms. I always thought that she would be very good at complaining in restaurants or shops. To make the point here is a snap of her below at the dining table.

Coco, just giving her unflattering opinion on the starter. Note the rather earnest and determined look: "This just won't do old chap!"

These feline dining experiences do not occur if we have any guests and, anyway, Leo does not mingle with visitors. Sometimes he will come to the bottom of the stairs to see who is here. But there is no danger of him butting in. Coco also tends to leave us in peace when visitors call, unless it is her beloved Mikey, the cat sitter. I have to confess that generally I like our little dining soirees with the cats. Their table manners being somewhat better than those of some of my old school friends, who come to visit.

Match of the Day

We are not great television watchers in our house, but Leo and Coco love to watch the "box". Although their choice of programmes is very different. Leo loves animal documentaries. If David Attenborough is on he will sit next to Benita on the sofa and give the TV his undivided attention for up to an hour at least. Of course, we have no real clue as to what he is making of it, but he appears to be sitting there and taking it all in. By which I mean that he looks at the screen very intently and seems to follow action sequences with his eyes. It is very strange to watch and doubtless causes us to engage in some anthropomorhic fantasy. But to all intents and purposed he appears to watch TV. Maybe this is not so strange. At Longleat Safari Park, when they first acquired a gorilla, the poor animal was showing many signs of loneliness and stress. But some years ago the senior keeper there told me that the poor fellow had been given a TV in his den and that this had solved the problem. I didn't ask what his favourite viewing was.

With Coco it's much clearer what she is up to. Coco loves soccer, but she watches in a very unique way. When football is on the TV Coco jumps onto the TV unit and presses her nose hard up against the screen. As the ball is hoofed around the pitch she follows it intently, moving her head along the trajectory of the ball. In exciting games, when the ball is moved around very fast, she actually jumps to try and catch the ball. But she is fussy about the style of play. Officianados of the beautiful game will be disappointed that she does not like to watch Spain. She has no time for that slow build up from the back. She is more of a Bolton Wanderer's girl, as she likes to see the long ball booted in the opposition penalty area. She quite likes watching England, because when England attack they give the ball away and it is belted down the pitch again. She loves end to end football. She is not keen on Italy, Argentina or Spain, but likes Germany and Manchester United. West Ham bring tears to her eyes.

The football interest is not surprising as Coco and Leo both play soccer in their own unique ways. Coco is a cracking goalie. Some readers may remember that Peter Bonetti, the former Chelsea goal keeper, was known as "the cat". But Coco is in a different league. Coco likes us to throw a rolled up ball of paper towards her so that she can jump and parry the paper ball with her paws. She literally flies through the air and never misses, just like a goalie pushing the ball over the bar or around the post. Unlike Mr Bonetti, who once had a less than glorious night in a World Cup quarter final against West Germany, she is rock solid.

Leo is more of a Stanley Matthews or Johan Cruyff. Leo will get a round object and dribble it down the kitchen or hallway at lightening speed, flicking it at high speed from paw to paw and never losing control of the ball. When I think how bad the ball control is in the England team, this brings tears to my eyes. Yes, a little Siamese cat is better with the ball than Beckham, Gerrard and Lampard etc. and he is on a fraction of the wages. Mind you, some of his antics would not be tolerated on the football pitch. After a devastasting dribble, he often throws the ball in the air and catches it in his mouth and runs off at max speed like a maniac. He seems to lose concentration and forgets what he is doing. As a supporter of West Ham United this behaviour is not unknown to me. Although even Paolo di Canio, who once picked the ball up to stop the game, never put it into in his mouth. Conversely, Leo has never pushed a referee over.

6

Off to North Somerset

Maybe you reach a certain age where you want to get out of the city. By 2009, after ten years in Frenchay, a suburb of Bristol, we were getting fed up of the traffic and congestion. In fact technically we lived in a village, but the north side of Bristol had grown into it and swallowed it. In itself it was an atractive place, however, new developments were springing up all over north Bristol and our village idyll was completely surrounded and increasingly hard to get out of. In our road many newcomers were remodelling the houses they had bought and it was like living on a building site. Some residents with large gardens were even having entirely new houses built in their grounds. And they want to relax the planning laws! But there were many irritants at work in our decision. Benita's journey to work was only two and a half miles, but was taking nearly an hour on some days. So for all kind of reasons, including the fact that someone had shot at Lucky, we decided to take our menage out to North Somerset. The Lawrences, Siamese included, were off.

Perhaps I should mention that by this time we had discovered the cottage in Rowberrow, where Doreen Tovey had lived. We did have some romantic notions of living near Rowberrow, but in fact it's a long commute from there to Bristol. And to be really honest the actual valley where Doreen lived, in what had been a miner's cottage, was rather damp and cold. So we settled on a little village in the Chew Valley, not many miles from where Doreen and René (Charles in the cat books) had lived before they moved to Rowberrow. To our dismay we learned that the Tovey's cottage had been bought by a couple who wanted to redevelop it into some kind of eco house. In fact five years later the place is now a wreck and will certainly be knocked down, which is a great shame. Still, in our Chew Valley house, we knew that it would be just 15 minutes to Rowberrow. So we believed we would be close to our beloved heroine of cat literature. Also her ashes were scattered opposite the cottage in Rowberrow and many of the cat heroes and heroines of the books were buried there as well. Rowberrow would become a place of pilgrimage for us.

The question of Leo

It was exciting to be off to the country, but we knew that we were in for some gyp with Leo. He did not like the fact that we were moving at all. In fact, as we now know very well, he hates change of any kind. Leo is a cat who essentially sees humanity as involved in a group conspiracy to commit murder against one Leo Stringfellow Lawrence Esq. He particularly doesn't like packing of any kind, boxes, loud noises, changes to normal routine, visitors, late phone calls etc. So as plans to move developed apace and boxes appeared and packing commenced, Leo was not a "happy bunny". All of which meant that we were increasingly non-plussed by the question of how one of us might actually capture him and get him into a cat box on the day of removal.

We were pinning our hopes on a honey trap, involving roast chicken. In this case a whole one. We hoped the smell and aroma of butter basted chicken with paprika would make Leo more docile and compliant and allow us to sneak up on him undetected. But as events were to show this was naïve. Leo had turned suspicion and doubt into an art form. He would be a natural for either MI5 or HMRC. As it turned out he could spot the difference between chicken as food and chicken as entrapment a mile off. So, despite inclement weather and the small matter of a grand piano to shift, the key hurdle to a successful move to the Chew Valley turned out to be a 5kg black cat, who had decided that he was "goin nowhere, no how, no way". Benita was incredibly stressed by the whole business and as the countdown commenced to moving, neither of us were confident that Leo would ever get to see Somerset. He had gone to ground and we rarely saw him from one day to the next. Coco, meanwhile, who is the most balanced of individuals, was taking it all in her stride. Nothing ruffles Coco, especially if grub and a comfortable place to sleep are available. Coco is like one of those fortunate people who sleep through severe turbulence on aircraft and open their eyes oblivious to the distress of their fellow passengers. Cool as a cucumber is Ms. Chanel.

Leo, looking uncannily like a characters from Harry Potter. This is an intelligent and resourceful cat and he does not like moving house. This is his "I am not very happy look". How could we get him into his cat box and out to Somerset?

North Somerset

On a very snowy day at the end of 2009 we and our possesions and two cats moved out to the Chew Valley. Sophisticated plans to trap Leo, by cooking a whole roast chicken came to nought. Although Leo sees chicken as a kind of opiate and it normally tranquillises him, he wasn't fooled by our ploy of placing a cooked chicken in the kitchen and then sneaking up on him when he was gastronomically engrossed. He wouldn't go anywhere near it, so in the end, when the house was completely empty and there was nowhere left to hide, we just ran him to ground in a corner and pounced. This took about four hours and we were all exhausted, including our neurotic feline. There was no wall of death routine this time and I think the weeks of us packing and all the noise had just run him down psychologically. He seemed to be resigned to the fact of being captured and taken to a place of execution. In the end we had used a rather crude and forceful capture process. But one that worked. And we were all at the end of our patience. A house move at Christmas, in deep snow, is a great recipe for maximum stress. As I staggered out of the door carrying one corner of a grand piano I wondered what the heck we were doing moving in the middle of a blizzard.

There then ensued a farcical series of events that would have done justice to one of the more insane moments in a Doreen Tovey book. One of our cars was a nice, but somewhat elderly convertible. I decided that, even this most non-functional of vehicles, would have to take some of the smaller items that we had not entrusted to the removal men. In order to pack stuff on the back seat I put the roof down for easier access and also so that I could see what I was doing. I got everything in, including Coco in her cat box on the passenger seat, and then got back into the car to close the roof. And guess what? The roof jammed. Then, just at that moment, another heavy snow storm commenced. It was just perfect, me and a forlorn Siamese cat sitting in the road in an open top car in a blizzard. So yes! The obvious thing was to get the car back in the garage pretty sharpish, except that I quickly remembered that the garage was now choc full of items that we were putting into storage.

So Coco and I were stuck out on the road in a cabriolet with the roof down in a snow storm. After a bit of cursing my luck I had a brainwave and quickly decided to ask a neighbour if I could put the dratted car in his garage. And he very kindly removed his and let me get our jalopy under shelter. But the snow was not stopping and we had to meet the removal truck in Chew in less than an hour. So we reversed the car out and I and Coco had to drive through Bristol and out to the Chew Valley in an open top car in a snow storm. I put a blanket over Coco's cage and I wore an old flying jacket and a wide brimmed hat, like a stetson. We got some amazing looks from people when we stopped at lights or were stuck in traffic. I decided to wave at people, trying to suggest that maybe I was participating in some bizarre motoring event or charity fund raising stunt for cats. But I think most onlookers just decided that I was a mad eccentric; someone keen on bracing weather and Siamese cats.

Despite my most uncomfortable trip out to North Somerset with Coco, the only issue that really concerned us was how our other nervous, not to say neurotic feline, would adapt to a new house. As is often said cats prefer their houses to their owners and are highly territorial. How would the little darlings like North Somerset? In fact the cat from Hogwart's School adapted much quicker than we did. And within three days both cats behaved as though they had lived at the new house for ever. As expected Coco took it all in her stride and, of course, Germans are known for being adaptable. The house was very cat friendly, with many large window sills and bays with seating areas to look through. Also a giant 30ft long living room where Siamese could accelerate to max speed and charge around totally uninhibited. The Siamese duo had given the new place the thumbs up.

The decorators

Our new house was in pretty good nick, but needed an odd lick of paint here and there. But I have never been very lucky at choosing tradesmen and in selecting someone to decorate the house I again revealed my poor judgement in personnel selection. Terry, was a large, talkative and very macho gentlemen from South Gloucestershire, who I had seen working on other houses in our road in Frenchay. I gave him a call and he seemed likeable enough. Although, people are crafty aren't they? After I hired him he only revealed his enthusiasm for Ghengis Khan, Nick Griffin and Hitler to me gradually. He also hid his dislike of cats. But yes! Yours truly selected Terry and his sidekick, Bob, (not the Likely Lads) to do our decorating.

Bob was a much more self effacing and quiet individual than Terry, and, it must be said, a good decorator. But he did have two critical weaknesses; he broke things and he liked long tea breaks. When Bob arrived on site, he began the day with a 20 minute tea break and perusal of the Sun newspaper in his van. Even more bizarrely he would take a 20 minute break at 4pm, before doing a final 30 minutes prior to finally downing tools for the day. He was a pleasant soul, but clumsy. Bob saw off a crystal decanter, a corner unit, the feet on a HiFi unit, wine glasses and a few other things for good measure. Mind you Terry made it clear that it was my fault. As he used to say, "But Phil, if they hadn't been left there he couldn't have broke em, could he". The logic was incontrovertible, so how could I argue? To be fair to Terry, he was in many ways a helpful soul and although he did actually not like decorating, he did sort out a few other jobs for us. It was some time before I realised that personality wise he was a cross between Arnold Schwarzenegger and Bernard Manning.

Terry often told me that we spoiled the cats rotten and that "we must be daft the money we spent on them". He used to give Coco some nasty looks and I would not have trusted him in the house if we had been absent. So in typical cat fashion Coco made a beeline for him. When Terry and Bob were at their ease, drinking a cuppa, Coco would go and jump on Terry's lap. With me watching Terry would have to grin and bear it and make entirely fake cooing noises to Coco. We have seen the cats do this before, often with people who are nervous of felines. One of my old school friends was pinned to the sofa for three hours once by Lucky, who just sat mute on Richard's chest. We returned from a shopping trip and asked our visitor if he was OK?. He replied that he was "desperate to go the loo", but terrified to move. Such is the power of the cat. But that wouldn't have worked with Terry, who I knew was desperate to swing a foot in Coco's direction.

As well as anti-catism and sympathy for proto fascism, Terry also had a strange sense of humour. One very snowy day he and Bob were working at our new house in the Chew Valley just prior to us moving in. When I popped over to see the progress being made I thought I was getting some strange looks from our new neighbours, but no one said anything. And then I realised that Terry and Bob had built a large snowman, or so I thought, on the back lawn. When I actually got around to looking outside I found that this was not in fact a snowman, but rather a large (6ft high) and uncannily accurate sculpture of the male reproductive organ. I had to let Terry "go" as they say in personnel circles. I believe he is now decorating at the Tate Modern.

Coco and the birds

When she was a kitten Coco had learned to walk on a harness and this was a practice that we revived in North Somerset. Despite Somerset being rural, it is quite industrialised re traffic, with many agricultural, quarrying and waste management vehicles on the road. We wanted Coco to acclimatise before she was let out on her own. Leo, we decided, was too nervy to go out. So the Lawrences and Coco Chanel began to explore the local lanes and meet some of the animals in the neighbourhood. Coco appeared to enjoy these sojourns and would amber along quite nonchalantly. Generally we only had to be cautious if we encountered someone with a large dog.

At the new house we were not far from a large lake where many acquatic bird varieties can be seen, including exotic migrants as well as Mallard, Coote, Canada Geese, Mute Swans etc. One day we put Coco on her lead and went down in the car to park by the lake and let Coco have a stroll. Ms. Chanel had handled dogs ok, but was not keen on the bird life. In Coco's eyes birds were clearly meant to be small creatures hopping about in the garden waiting to be caught by the fierce and daring feline predator. But these birds were 4 or even 6 times Coco's size. One day a huge Canada Goose came close to our Siamese princess and gave her a wing flap and a few shrill screetches. Coco jumped back behind my legs and started howling that it was time to get out of this horrible place. So back we went home never to return with Coco to the banks of Chew Lake and the giant, fierce birds. From then on Coco just watched the doves, sparrows and blue tits in our garden, chuntering all kinds of threats at them, but never being allowed to do any harm. I am sure Bill Oddy and Chris Packham would approve. Leo was not a problem on the bird front and had no desire to venture out, as in his view outside there were hordes of terrorists; mountebanks and cat kidnappers; only poultry, either enroute to or from an oven, interested him. If given a vote on best Englishman we are sure he would go for Bernard Matthews.

Coco, safe back at home, but somewhat traumatized by her experience down at Chew Lake. From now on birds meant sparrows and starlings period!

The cat that stopped the clock

A new little Siamese game started at the new Chew Valley house concerning Coco and a clock. We own quite an attractive, antique Dutch wall clock, and its swinging pendulum mesmerises Coco. In Frenchay it was positioned out of reach, but in Chew it was adjacent to the corner of our dining table and not far above an old wooden bureau. Coco started to sit and watch the clock for hours on end. I also noticed that her expression was one of annoyance. In fact she was glaring at the clock as though it was her greatest enemy. Despite the fact that Siamese have a reputation for being a little eccentric in their behaviour, I was rather puzzled by this. But I eventually concluded that Coco just does not like clocks, especially clocks with visible and noisy pendulums. At our previous house the clock was not really vulnerable to feline sabotage, Coco would watch it for hours, but could not get at it. However, now at the Chew house we found that the clock kept stopping. Although it was clear that Coco's glares were not the cause I decided that there must be some Siamese trickery at work here. We did have it checked over just to make sure, but no fault was found. So what was making the clock stop?

*The antique dutch clock that Coco stopped. It's 2:30pm,
not Chinese dentist time, but Coco time!*

After the check over we put it back on the wall, set it going and awaited the result. We are rather fond of this clock and were disappointed to find that it was just the same; it would run for a period and then it kept stopping. Every day we set it and every day it stopped. But then we started to monitor it and we discovered the answer. On a particular day we set the clock and, as we had visitors for dinner, laid the table and closed the dining room door to keep feline marauders at bay. Perhaps I should add that our "meezers" like to play a little game when we lay the table. This consists of getting under the table cloth and playing "ghosts" by running up and down howling and having a pretend fight. So it's a good idea all round to keep them out when preparing the dining room. This time it also allowed us to diagnose the cause of our broken clock. With no Siamese present we noticed that by early evening our beloved clock was ticking away merrily. And then the penny dropped.

During dinner Coco popped in to inspect the guests. Focusing of course, in the classical feline style, on a man who does not like cats. Then she noticed that the clock was ticking. Quick as a flash she jumped onto the top of the bureau close to the end of the table, studied the clock for a few seconds and then put up her left forepaw and stopped the pendulum. She turned, jumped down and gave us a "mission accomplished" look and trotted out of the room. This was done with great insouciance; she didn't like the noise of the clock and she darn well stopped it. So the problem with the clock was not mechanical, but rather feline intervention. We have since tested the hypothesis by setting the clock and observing the behaviour of our little princess, known locally as "the Minx". Without fail Coco immediately climbs on the bureau, stretches up the wall and puts her paw out to stop the pendulum. We just leave the door closed now.

The thief of Baghdad

Different Siamese cats offer their owners a choice of contrasting eccentric behaviours. While Coco attacks various machines, Leo is a terrible thief. Well, in fact, a very good thief. Just recently I found some sausage rolls mauled to death on the hall floor. But over the years he has pulled off some remarkable feats of culinary larceny. To be on the safe side you can't leave any source of protein unattended in the kitchen. Sausages, duck breasts, ham sandwiches and chicken rolls have all been pilfered. If you're having a "running lunch" and make the mistake of putting a sandwich down when Leo is around then it is goodbye to your grub, not au revoire. At the new house in Chew our cat burglar took larceny to new levels. One incident stands out in my memory. Back in 2011 we had entertained one day for Sunday lunch and cooked a leg of lamb. Despite our best efforts there was a good deal of meat left on the joint after lunch and I decided that I would strip it and, being a bit of a dab hand with curry, try and make a lamb rogan josh. I had begun this task on the following Monday and was chopping away in the kitchen when the telephone rang and I went into the hall to answer. I became rather engrossed in the call and was on the telephone for about 20 minutes. When I had finished I needed to find some papers to answer a query posed by the caller and I left the kitchen unattended to go to the study.

When I returned the leg of lamb was gone. Then from the corner of my eye I saw a black object flash by with what looked like a little dumb-bell in its mouth. The impression on my senses was just a blur and did not become comprehensible for a few seconds until the truth dawned on me. Yes, the thief of Baghdad had run off with the meat for my curry masterpiece! As with their big cousins in the wild, domestic cats will take a piece of prey or food off to somewhere safe where they can eat in private or save it for later. Leo, I think, had not found a satisfactory hide, so for the next five minutes I pursued him like Inspector Clouseau around the house. Eventually he dropped the lamb in the hallway and scurried off upstairs looking very aggrieved. The lamb had not fared well so rogan josh was off.

The pilfered lamb was not the only feline felony. With Leo being such a chicken addict, we had given up on drumsticks and thighs and were roasting a whole chicken about every 6 days or so. Being superstitious we kept the wish bones to break and make the customary exhortation for good luck. They were piling up in a kitchen cupboard as we had run out of obvious wishes. One day I returned home and noticed that something was crunching under my feet on the kitchen tiles. A closer inspection revealed this material to be ground up bones. For a minute I thought some poor little mammal had entered the house and suffered a grim demise at the hands of the Siamese savages. But then I noticed that a cupboard door was open and I realised that this detritus was the wishbone stock pile that Leo had managed to extract from the cupboard and ground up in his teeth. Nothing was safe, and Siamese being what they are, a closed door was no protection. Anything vaguely reminiscent of protein had to be locked away.

And it is not just food. Leo also likes to take shiny things like jewellery and sometimes pens. Back in Frenchay one of Benita's most expensive rings disappeared. This was an 18ct gold sapphire diamond cluster and worth a few bob. After a few weeks of searching we had more or less given up on finding it and then it turned up under the bed that Leo sleeps on during a Spring clean. He is like a magpie and loves bright things. But he's very neat and orderly. On another occasion I was working on some papers in the dining room and my pens kept disappearing. Then, as with the lamb, I noticed the black shadow flash by with a black object clamped in his mouth. On pursuing him to his lair I discovered 4 pens nicely lined up together and well chewed at the end. The joy of Siamese.

Un peu de cinq à sept avec une chat

At the time that we moved into the Chew Valley I had left academia and was working in Toulouse for a leading aircraft manufacturer as an economist. We had a little country house about 40 miles from Toulouse near the town of Gaillac, where I stayed. It was a lonely time and I missed our little meezers (and Benita) very much. But I am afraid that I was unfaithful to Coco. The French have a little saying about a man who visits his mistress after work for a couple of hours on the way home. They call it cinq-a-sept (five to seven). Of course this is very convenient and practical as it does not completely deprive the wife and family of the man's company in the evening. And there is a nice convenient cover; "I was working late" is a readymade excuse to hide a little triste with une femme d'amour. It is all very French, although in Quebec it really does mean a meeting or gathering after work.

Well, in my lonely sojourn in Gaillac, I suddenly found that I had early evening company. A charming and tiny female cat started to come and stare through the French windows on the terrace about 6:30pm-7:00 pm every night. She was petite to a fault and very nervous and coquettish. She had a slightly tabby looking head and a lovely cream and caramel cost. Eventually, after a few weeks coaxing, she would come inside the house for 5 or 10 minutes, but no longer. Of course I started to feed her and gradually we developed an enduring relationship. Unlike the Siamese she liked milk and cream and would lap it up with relish on the terrace. She was painfully thin and I was glad to be able to give her some food. She didn't say much, but had a very squeaky and endearing high pitched voice. She did not like me to close the windows when she came into the house, so even in deepest winter her visits meant the French windows had to be left open.

Lady's early evening visit became a highlight of the day for me, especially as I didn't tend to see any people after I left the office in Toulouse. My French colleagues tended to socialize at lunchtime, but were always keen to get home at night. My social life revolved around my petite chat. I never tracked down where she came from. She was not feral, but not really domesticated either. Possibly she lived on one of the local farms. Sadly, I could not adopt her properly as I was back in the UK every weekend and also knew that my

Ma Petite Chat! Lady, my French feline mistress rolling over in pleasure on the terrace. I decided not to tell Coco.

period in France was limited. I named her Lady, which seemed rather unimaginative, but somewhat appropriate as that is exactly what she was. Benita also got to know her on odd weekend visits, but agreed with me that Coco must be kept in the dark. Siamese are funny, beautiful, loyal and make great companions, but also jealous and possessive.

We were blessed with Lady's company for nearly a couple of years and then suddenly she disappeared and was never seen again. I must say that I feared the worst, as the local environment had many animals that might prey on a cat. Dead cats were also a common sight on the local roads and indeed, I buried quite a few in our garden alongside some rabbits. To my horror I had found that some of the rabbits in the local area had myxomatosis. I have no idea if it was natural or had been artificially introduced, but it is a horrible and cruel disease. If I discovered an infected rabbit I always took them to the local vet in Gaillac. A charming man who had studied in Dublin and had the most extraordinary Irish accent when he spoke English. He would put the poor mites to sleep and I would take them home and bury them under a lime tree.

Paradise Lost or other people are hell (said Jean-Paul Satre)

In Gaillac life was peaceful, but also very lonely. I used to daydream about being back in the West Country with the Siamese duo. I had actually spent very little time at the Chew house. North Somerset seemed idyllic and the cats loved it at first, but sadly things began to change very quickly.

At this time, as I have already mentioned, I was commuting on a weekly basis by air to work in Toulouse. In France I had a 90 mile round trip every day between our house in Gaillac and my employer's office near Toulouse airport. So weekends back in Somerset needed to offer good R&R to enable me to recover from the week's exertions. But this much needed peace and relaxation was not to be had, and, as we shall see, I became the victim of a vicious cement mixer and raucous soccer players.

Our new country house was quite modern and had been built alongside five or six other detached houses in a seemingly quiet village lane. But to be blunt, because developers today are often quite greedy, we were a little bit sandwiched in between the two properties that belonged to our imediate neighbours on either side. In fact six houses had been built in our lane by the father of our immediate neighbour, who was an engineer turned builder. But really the space should have accommodated just four houses and, as we discovered, close proximity would lead to conflict with the builder's son and our neighbours further up the lane; we had double trouble!

On one side of our house, just up the lane, there was a nice family with four teeenage boys. At first relations were cordial, but the lads played football in the garden and had actually installed proper goals. These lads were soccer crazy and their Dad was a fanatical Everton supporter. Other boys from the village, and

70

sometimes even adults, would join them in the late afternoon for games of four or five-a-side. So, despite the fact that the folks next door were likeable, we were concerned that there was a lot of noise, especially of the ball being whacked very hard against the fence that ran alongside our living room external wall. Even worse, occasionally, the ball would come over the fence and whack into our large bay windows, which curved out into the garden. Our nervy Siamese did not like this and would wince when there was an impact. And in fact we were concerned that the windows might actually break. These were big lads, not little toddlers, and they gave the ball a mighty thwack. Our particular neurosis was that they might break the window whilst we were out and that the cats might get out.

Over and above the issues with the cats I have to admit that as time went by I was also getting irritated just by the noisy soccer itself. On some evenings in the summer the noise just became unbearable. So gradually one of those sad and typical stories of modern life ensued. I complained more and more vociferously about the "racket" and gradually relations became strained and not very cordial. Apologies were made, but nothing ever changed. Sometimes the whole family and the boys' girlfriends would have a kick about and the ball would regularly pound against our window. The cat's didn't like it and neither did I. It was all very stressful as I knew we were heading towards a major confrontation.

And then one summer evening, during a family kick about, the worst happened. The ball thundered into the French windows and broke the glass. I have to confess, that as the modern idiom has it, I just "lost it". I went around there to Little Goodison like a man possessed and had a good rant, scream and shout about "irresponsible, stupid people and the end of civilisation" etc. etc. They were rather stunned and very apologetic and I found the whole thing utterly distressing, as I actually liked this family a great deal. But until the broken window episode I just could not get them to see that the noise was unacceptable. As Leo rightly says, noisy neighbours are one of the curses of modern life.

But this was only half of the problem, as on the other side of our property the son of the builder of our house turned out to be a DIY freak. Someone who would go out on a Sunday morning and start cutting bricks with a grinder or power up his cement mixer, just as we were serving our Sunday lunch. We had visitors sometimes from London, who would joke that they were going back to the "smoke" for a rest. We were getting very stressed. Our country idyll had Goodison Park on one side and Barratt Homes on the other. The cats, especially Leo, did not like the sound of the power tools at all. In fact he (and I) were now finding the Chew Valley countryside not to be all it was cracked up to be. In our new house the sound of electric saws, petrol driven hedge trimmers, shredding machines and other infernal devices was ever present and it drove Leo and I nuts.

Sometimes I wonder how we managed in the age before petrol engined leaf vacuums and turbo-charged jet washers. No Siamese cat wants to live next door to "Bob the Builder". Leo is like me, he hates DIY; he likes people who read books, sip glasses of wine, play bridge, listen to Schubert, indeed, any peaceful or cerebral activity. Leo and I both believe in live and let live. But while some peoples' activities are essentially private, others pursue very invasive hobbies and life-style choices. I started to ponder whether Leo and I could remain at the Chew Valley house. But I didn't fancy telling my long suffering wife that we might be on the move again. But have you noticed that what sometimes starts out as inconceivable can quickly become a very probable course of action. This process did not take long.

But one clutches at straws. Looking at our neighbour's house, which was huge and had been extended three times, it was hard to see where the next building project could be undertaken and we lived in hope. But we were wrong in this surmise and, as we discovered, even a nice patio needs to be relaid, a lawn needs a concrete footpath across the middle, a rough area where tools are stored needs concrete slabs putting down and a new wood burner needs a new chimney erecting etc. etc. So in fact it was clear that Monsieur Bricolage was never going to stop. One summer evening our charming neighbour started cutting bricks about 8pm, right next to our mutual hedge.

The dust was blowing into our garden and settling on clothes that were on the washing line. Yet another pointless and fractious discussion ended with me learning that Tony (my neighbour) saw it as his right to pursue home improvement at any time he chose.

And there were other little things. For reasons that elude me Monsieur Bricolage would go out after dark and proceed to reposition the family's three cars. This was noisy, but the worst aspect was that the headlight beams shone through our windows. Our main bedroom had a side window opposite Tony's parking area and sometimes, around 11pm, our bedroom would be illuminated like the auditorium during a Pink Floyd concert. If I was asleep this would really unhinge me as it was as though a police or FBI marksman was lining up a shot. It also woke Leo and Coco, whose bedroom was right opposite the dodgem cars. All very strange and, as I have since spoken to the brave man who bought our Chew house, I know that this odd little ritual continues. People really are weird. And I can hardly talk as I have let my life be taken over by Siamese cats. I can't be much of a man either as I get no pleasure from a trip to B&Q or a builders' merchant. Mind you I don't go out and wash my cars in the rain. Guess who did that?

Off again

All things considered I now knew that we would have to move yet again. Even I started to believe the family taunts about gypsy blood. And yet there must be readers that know what I mean. People can be utter hell. Benita was livid with me, but I (and Leo) were now adamant that, even though it was within one year of our move out of Bristol, we would have to up sticks again. Coco hates inconvenience but came around to Leo's view and that was enough for me. Leo thought the builder was completely mad and, as they say, it takes one to know one.

Of course I did remonstrate with the gentlemen concerned on several more occasions and pointed out that he was breaking local authority regulations. But, as he explained to me yet again, he was busy running his plumbing business during the week, so evening and weekends were the only time that he could do this work. I wanted to say that maybe he should get some ark lights and work all the way through the night. But you never know do you? He just might have thought that I was serious. So I just said that I understood fully and immediately put our house on the market. I just wondered if I could look someone in the eye and encourage them to buy our property. Regrettably the agent insisted that we could not put, "would suit purchaser with hearing disability" in the ad for the house. In fact a smashing family did buy the house and my guilt was assuaged by the fact that they were desperate to get their daughter onto the roll for the local school, which has a very strong reputation. Such is the real currency of today's property market for parents who care about their kid's education.

However, after all of this I was still feeling very guilty. My insanity had actually reached new levels as at the same time as disposing of the Chew house I had more or less by accident managed to sell our house in Gaillac, near Toulouse. The dreaded packing started again in two houses simultaneously in two different countries. I started to dream about 50cm cubed cardboard packing cases. Poor old Leo was freaked out. Mr and Mrs Lawrence were not doing too well either. The housing market had gone down and we were told that we would lose £25,000 on the Chew house. And, of course, we were also looking at another £20,000 plus stamp duty fee. I have to say that I find stamp duty the most annoying of taxes and paying it twice in two years is a bit much. But then something happened that cheered me up and also amazed and titilated our friends. It even helped with the stress. Although it was also quite spooky.

Kismet

Readers may recall that back in 1998 we had bought our Bristol house from a charming couple called the Dewhursts. They had been wonderful to deal with and had left the house in great condition and had helped us enormously, by organising all the paperwork and keys for the house in the most efficient way. They were the dream vendors of a house; friendly, efficient and honest to a fault. Now fate took a hand.

We had been searching the local agent's sites for a couple of months to no avail and wondered if we would have to grin and bear it in Chew for a while. Then, one day in desperation, I was scanning the ads of agents further afield, around the Mendips in fact, when I saw a house that appealed to me in an attractive village on the Mendip Edge. I called the agents in Congresbury and booked a viewing for the following Saturday. I vaguely remembered that Jeff and Carol Dewhurst had moved out into Somerset, but we had not been in contact for 12 years and I had no idea where they lived.

We arrived at the property, which looked very promising and the lady from Fry and Baxter said she would just check if Mr and Mrs Dewhurst were at home. No penny dropped at this point, as we were avidly viewing the lovely garden and orchard. We ambled over to the front door, where the agent was already in conversation with the vendor. Then, to my utter astonishment, I realised that it was Jeff Dewhurst standing in the doorway. A little bit greyer and thicker around the waist than 13 years earlier, but definitely J. Dewhurst esquire. We both did a huge double take and struggled to say anything coherent. He regained his composure first and calmly said, "Hello Philip, Hello Benita, what a surprise!"

We were both stunned and tried to explain to the agent that we had purchased a house from the same vendors before back in 1998, but she seemd not to understand. Anyway… gradually some normality returned and we chatted in a buzz of excitement about this amazing co-incidence. I already knew that I liked the house and that there was a real possibility of buying twice from the same vendors. I wondered how often this happened. Of course I was convinced that this was Kismet, that fate had decreed it. And it meant that my cock-up of buying the Chew House, with the neighbours from hell, could be quickly forgotten. The Glebe, as it is called, also looked a perfect house for a couple of Siamese rogues and there was room for a large cat run in the garden. There was also a lovely fish pond and an orchard; all things we had never experienced before. I was utterly ecstatic. *We were always meant to buy the Dewhurst house*! So needless to say we had to proceed. The trouble was the Dewhurst's also knew that we were hooked. This time they were a little more ruthless about the price and the terms and conditions. When kismet is driving a house purchase negotiation is difficult. We were putty in the agent's hands.

7

Somerset Siamese

The Dewhursts were very settled into village life and pillars of the local church. However, they had grandchildren up in the Midlands, who they rarely got to see. After 12 years in Somerset they were going back to their roots in Worcestershire. They were sad to be leaving the Mendips, but keen to be re-united with their family. We saw ourselves as the lucky ones as good had come out of bad and our next (and hopefully final) move meant that we ended up in a lovely house very close to where Doreeen Tovey had lived. Thus in 2011, 18 months after moving to the Chew Valley, we went another 8 miles south west onto the edge of the Mendips, about four miles from where Doreen had lived in Rowberrow. Of couse the whole malarkey with the cats was repeated and Leo was even harder to trap this time. But we were now hardened movers and not about to take any truck (only the removal lorry). When we moved we left a double bed in the room where the cats used to sleep, which was to go the council tip. Having chased Leo around the house for 4 hours he finally retreated like an exhausted outlaw under this bed. I reached under again and again to grab him and he moved away from my grasp. Eventually, I became utterly exasperated with this and I lifted the bed up vertically on its end so that Benita could grab the little blighter. He was in the cage and we were off. Now we really had taken the Siamese to Somerset.

Mendip (Siam) meezers

The Mendips are lovely; one of those few places left in England that is still quite wild and unspoilt. The hills only rise to about 1000 ft, but in places there are grand views of the Bristol Channel and Wales beyond. Our new house (where we still live!) is in a village on the Mendip Edge, with wooded slopes and pasture land to one side and a large lake, renowned for its trout, on the other. The local countryside is full of interesting fauna; including peregrine falcons, fallow deer, adders, giant blue butterflies and rare species of bats. Those who remember Doreen Tovey's books may recall that one of her persistent fears was that of adders biting her cats. Fortunately, where we are, they are not so common as down in the valley at Rowberrow.

The cats took to our new house very easily, as they had done in the Chew Valley. The new place was bigger and offered plenty of room for mad Siamese to charge about. One "course" took our feline gallopers out of the breakfast room, through the kitchen, along the hallway, upstairs and along the landing and into a bedroom we call the "long room", as it is narrow, but 25ft in length; altogether about a 40 metre sprint. When this cat derby ensues the noise is quite incredible, as both Leo and Coco are large and heavy cats (now both about 6 kilos). Doreen's Siamese steeplechase is alive and well in the Mendips.

The larger house was important as, apart from the occasional walk on a lead for Coco, the cats now lived inside. With our precious Lucky having been shot by an airgun back in Bristol and with many foxes and other predators in our new environment, we weren't going to take any chances. But to give them some fresh air we had a large outside cat run built next to the garage. Although this proved to be of limited value, as when we put Coco in it she screamed the place down and clearly preferred to be indoors. Coco, as her name suggests, is a lady who likes her comforts. In the last year or so her waistline has rather spread and she is clearly an Epicurean and a bit of a hedonist by nature. I have to confess that I recently added the nickname "chuggs" to her various monikers. Having said that she can still sprint about the house and is surprisingly agile. Nevertheless, we have been given a firm dressing down by the nice people at the Bristol University Langford Small Animal Vetinary Practice (where

Doreen Tovey also took her tribe) about her weight. But we have a little problem as Coco, God bless here, is the first greedy cat that we have ever owned. Indeed, one prone to knocking the top off the butter and tucking into some nice saturated fats, as well as stealing food from Leo. Mind you, regarding her size, one must remember that she is a "trad" and likely to be bulkier than the svelte modern that Leo represents. We are sure that really she is just "big boned", which is certainly how Coco likes to characterise herself. With the outside largely off limits, our little predators roam around the house

Coco Chanel (Chuggs) trying to work off some of her newly acquired ballast. You may be able to see that Leo does the same routine, but on the carpet which is fraying nicely!

seeking out flies, daddy longlegs, spiders and other insects to hunt and devour. The sight of Leo leaping up into the windows to clutch at flying insects is quite remarkable and sometimes a little alarming, if it happens without warning. Leo and Coco also like to sit on the window ledges, making strange threatening noises at passing birds and squirels. The squirrels thunder along a fence opposite the kitchen window. Our gardener, an ex anti-terrorism detective no less, calls the fence the "squirrel M5". They raid a bird feeder just opposite the kitchen and stare back nonchalantly at the two house bound Siamese. The chuntering noise Siamese make at enemies is quite strange; a kind of cross between chirping and clicking. One thing that is sure is that it's not meant to be friendly to potential prey; probably better all round that we don't know what is being said.

To ensure plenty of exercise the cats have toys that encourage running and jumping. Leo dribbles ping pong balls around the floors and Coco jumps up at little animals suspended on fishing rods. But of course a Siamese also has to relax. In the new house we saw very clearly how important windows are to indoor cats. Leo and Coco would sit for hours watching the fauna outside. Cats, big and small, are great watchers and I imagine, as hunters, show tremendous patience as they observe prey. This is yet another reason that I am so partial to felines; their ability to sit companiably for hours just doing nothing. Cats are not into "carpe diem", more like seize the sofa. In Latin that might be "rapere ad pedem". Someone once said that being lazy was resting when you are not tired. Cats would go for that as a mantra and good luck to them.

One of our squirrels just sauntering past on the M5. Coco is chuntering dire threats from the kitchen window.

Sometimes our wildlife viewing is quite exciting, both for us and the cats. The Somerset house has a large garden at the front and, as there are no street lights, we have infra-red sensor lights dotted around the drive and lawn in order to see when we exit or return to the property. One early morning at around 2am in the Spring of 2013 we noticed that the lights were being triggered very regularly and staying on for long periods. Also our little meezers were squawking away and clearly very agitated about something. So we crept very quietly into the main sitting room to have a sly peak through the window. What we saw really amazed us. A family of badgers were digging up the edge of the lawn by a large yew tree that stands on the right hand side of the garden. There were two adults and a youngster. But of course it was probably just sentimental to assume that they were a mum, dad and baby trio. We and the Siamese watched for about 30 minutes before they scuttled off into the darkness. Oddly enough the intrepid duo did not make a sound and seemed to recognise that badgers could not be prey. I have always liked badgers and I see them as a quintessentially English animal; one that we should be proud of. I didn't mind that they had done a bit of damage to the lawn. Probably the ultra wet winter had impacted quite strongly on their normal sources of food. They were just looking for some grub.

Sadly, these days they are not safe in our animal loving islands and also not as common in the UK as some people think. On the roads and lanes close to where we live we see many that have been run over and killed. It upsets me profoundly to see them just left to be minced up by passing traffic. If I can do so safely I often stop and move them onto the verge to give them a vestige of dignity. Our gardener tells me that some of them have been shot and are left on the road to cover up the slaying of a protected species. But as I write badgers are being culled in West Somerset as a "trial" in the battle against the spread of Bovine TB. But I think that the leading zoologist Lord Krebs has a strong case when he argues that the cull is virtually pointless. As Krebs contends even near extermination in specified areas does not lead to a huge reduction in tuberculosis. It's hard to accept that the cull conforms to the idea that the badgers are a protected species, imagine their plight otherwise. Sometimes I just wish they could fight back and hats off to Queen's Brian May for leading some resistance. He must also be a cat lover, like his former close friend the late Sir Patrick Moore. I recently heard someone say that the identities of the badger marksmen are being kept secret to ensure their safety. Maybe the badgers are planning revenge after all.

Pandamonium in the pub

Turning to a more cheerful subject, after the move to the Mendips we soon discovered that one of the great joys of our new village location was a real old-style pub, which, as well as good food and drink, offers a spectacular view of the local lake from its rear garden. This was a very pleasant first for me, as never before had I experienced the pleasure of having a decent pub within easy walking distance. So, to make use of this asset, in our second year in the village we got into the habit of popping into our wonderful hostelry on summer evenings, just for a quick half before going back for dinner. Little did we know that we were about to become notorious in the local inn. And yes! It did have something to do with Siamese.

Given Coco's expanding waistline and also the fact that the cats were now largely kept indoors, we decided to re-introduce the harnesss for short walks outside. Much to our surprise, Coco reacted very placidly to this new spell of walking on a lead. Unlike Leo she is actually very calm and easy going, "bomb-proof" as her breeder said, and a dream from a pet management point of view. She even enters the cat box of her own volition for trips to the vet. So we started having little strolls out in the garden and then graduated to strolling down the lane in the direction of the pub, which is only 250 yards away. On one balmy night in July we found ourselves opposite the pub at about 6:15pm. The garden seemed very quiet so we decided that a quick drink was not going to create any problems. We walked through the small car park and sat on a bench under a large beech tree, overlooking the lake. There were 3 or 4 other tables occupied and we did get some odd looks, but British reserve is a powerful force and no one commented on our Siamese companion. Coco setled down on the bench next to Benita and sat there as quiet as a mouse.

Gradually, a few more people arrived in the pub garden, but all was peace and tranquility. It was idyllic; a garden of Eden with no serpent in sight. The sun's rays were glinting off the surface of the lake, the temperature was a lovely low 20s and it was utterly relaxing to be sat there just sipping half of the local cider. But then a car pulled up and a couple climbed out pulling a sprightly Jack Russell on a lead. They came through the swing gate into the garden and sat at a table about 20ft away, but directly opposite. I like Jack Russells, but they are not a peaceful and retiscent type of animal. I just hoped that he would not see Coco. She seemed to tense up, but did not move or begin any hissing or growling.

For a couple of minutes all was well, but then Robbie, as he was called, saw Coco and began barking furiously. Coco jumped up onto Benita's lap. I thought it best that we drink up and get going as quick as we could. But we were too late. Robbie, who was on a telescopic lead, stole a march on his owner and jerked the lead from his master's hand. He then charged full tilt like a supercharged whippet across the grass towards our table. Coco let out a hell-cat scream and jumped upwards towards one of the overhanging branches on the tree above our bench. By this time Bob had landed on our table and knocked the drinks over. Coco had managed to get her front paws around a branch just behind where Benita was sitting. But her horizontal leap had wrapped the cat lead around Benita's neck. Coco hung there looking most undignified trying to get a better purchase in her sanctuary, while Robbie lunged up towards her trying to bite her rear end. It was all rather surreal.

This had all happened at lightning speed and initially I froze, not really grasping what had taken place. When I came to my senses I jumped up and grabbed Coco out of the branches, while Benita, non too gently, pushed Bob off our table. The next thing Robbie's owners were looming. I naively thought that a big apology was about to be offered, but in fact the first words I heard, in a thick Bristolian accent, were, 'What did you think would happen, bringin a cat like that down the pub'. Further belligerent comments suggested that Benita and I were 'stark raving bonkers'. I must admit that I was a bit rattled and made the mistake of trying to be smart. I said something on the lines of, 'Well! I didn't think we would be savaged by a psychotic Jack Russell'. It was all getting a little bit nasty.

But the pub staff came to our rescue. Fortunately, the kitchen at the pub overlooks the back garden, and the landlord's wife, Jean, had actually seen most of what transpired. She soon appeared and intervened on our behalf, confirming that Jack the Russell, was indeed the aggressor. I tried to chip in with the view that if Robbie *Sugar Ray* Russell had been under control the whole episode could not have occurred. But reason is futile in these situations. **Coco had provoked the attack**. I wondered if we had invented something called pet rage. We recovered our composure, finished our drinks and carried Coco home. I felt very guilty, first she was threatened by giant Canada geese and now she had been assaulted by a Jack Russell. She forgave me; **she's a good un that Coco**, slow to get angry and quick to give love. Up with the trads!

In time we saw the funny side of the episode and realised that maybe taking a Siamese to the local pub was not a great idea, especially when many dogs are taken into the garden. And no one came to any real harm, which is not always the case where dog incidents are concerned. It's all relative as they say: not long before a local landowner's Anatolian shepherd dogs escaped from their enclosure and nearly killed a woman visitor to a local beauty spot and, indeed, did kill the lady's poor German Shepherd. Domestic cats have their detractors, but they rarely cause serious injury and never maul people to death.

8

The Patter of Tiny Paws

Coco soon recovered from the assualt and battery. But after the episode at the pub we decided to limit her walks to just around the garden. This was somewhat restricted though, as our second winter in Somerset was one of the wettest I have ever known. Around the Mendips and the Chew Valley there was extensive flooding and a poor chap actually drowned in his car in a stream next to our our old house in Chew Village. Many of our local roads were like rivers, but we stayed safely indoors during the bad weather and just walked to our local and invaluable village store for provisions. And occasionally to the pub for a little infusion.

Eventually Spring did arrive and Coco started to explore our half an acre of garden on the lead. On the left, at the front of the house, we have a small orchard, with 6 apple trees and a couple of pears. This area is quite overgrown and Coco loves to go and have a rummage down there. Also this spot attracts a few of the village cats, who like to repose in the orchard having a snooze. One such is a big, long haired boy, called Georgeous. The lady who looks after him, Heather, told me that he is so named simply because he is gorgeous. But I discovered that, gorgeous or not, he is kept outside, as Heather's husband will not allow him in the house. I started thinking about naming humans according to looks or personality. And I must confess that a not very flattering nickname was coined for he who keeps Gorgeous out in the cold. Sometimes when Heather is away we feed this lovely old boy who slumbers in our orchard. He looks ok on his outdoor life and seems to also get food at some of the local farms. He always scarpers when we approach with Lady Chanel, but I think she has a soft spot for him. Another

visitor is a big ginger tom, called Bailey. He sits opposite the kitchen staring wistfully at the Siamese duo. Leo sometimes growls at him, but runs a mile if Bailey approaches the window. Leo is all talk.

As Spring matured and the weather improved Coco and Leo seemed very happy in our Mendips' hideout and, by any standards, were given very nice accommodations and a very attractive lifestyle. Their regime is essentially, sleep, eat, sleep, play, eat and sleep. The house is festooned with cat toys and scratching posts. And they even have their own feline version of scalextric, a game in which they propel a glass ball around a covered figure of 8 track, like a bobsleigh run. Leo, of course, takes the supposedly irremovable top off the track, removes the ball and hoofs it around against the skirting boards. Making a terrible racket.

Our luxury inclined boarders stay upstairs at night in what is exclusively their domain, as we have a bedroom and bathroom on the ground floor. Some may wonder why our cats are locked in a room at night, but letting Siamese roam free around the house means the sound of crashes and bangs and being serenaded in the middle of the night by those seeking succour, food and company. Back in Chew Valley we had given Leo and Coco free rein at night and at about 5am there would be a chorus outside our bedroom door demanding entry. In what some may consider a rather eccentric response, we would get up and go and sleep in the double bed in the cat's room. In effect we swapped bedrooms in the middle of the night. My theory was that this confused the cats and allowed us a couple more hours of sleep. Mrs Lawrence's theory was that I was bonkers.

These domestic arrangements could not last and we changed to a regime where the Siamese singers of the dawn were locked into their own bedroom. Even better, as I have said, their room is not on the same floor as our bedroom and we all get a decent night's sleep. This may seem mean, but suits us fine and ensures some peace. Also, we know that in a real emergency, we would hear old Leo foghorn a mile away. He's utterly adorable, but not a being you want to spend the night with. Some cats may be able to sleep on the bed with their owners, but not ours. Leo, who has been christened "Wriggle Bum" (actually something a little cruder) at the local vets, is a total fidget and needs his own space. So the cats have their bedroom and we have ours. They also have their own bedtime and don't like it if they are late. If we return from a late evening out, thus delaying the arrival of suppper, we are subject to severe and prolonged oriental vocal chastisement. Owning Siamese is a serious business.

Madness takes hold

Despite the peace and tranquility that had entered our new life in Somerset and the way that the two Siamese amigos had settled into the new routine, I succombed to further madness back in the Spring of 2012 and decided that a third cat might be a nice idea. After all: what could be better than two Siamese? Answer: three Siamese. As I adore seal points there was only one type of Siamese that I would consider and Benita and I both thought that a female would be less likely to upset the applecart with our neurotic little boy, Leo. But we knew that this was a risky business and Benita was much less sanguine about having a third Siamese. Back in the days of their first Siamese duo, Solomon and Sheba, Doreen and René Tovey had acquired a new male kitten called Samson. Things had not panned out well and Solomon and Sheba reacted with great hostility to the poor little mite who had been brought to the White Cottage at Rowberrow. In less than a week, although full of remorse, Doreen changed her mind and took the little fellow back to the breeder who she had bought him from. Peace was restored.

Without wanting to sound like a knowall, I believe that today, thanks to the work of modern animal behaviourists and zoologists like Peter Neville and John Bradshaw, we have a lot more scientifically valid information about cat behaviour and requirements than Doreen Tovey had access to back in the 1950s and 1960s. So I was hopeful that, with the correct procedures, we could introduce a kitten and that the in-situ cats would accept her. But there is no doubt that this is a risky business and that some pet owners don't grasp the difficulty of having multi-cat households and the stress that it generates. Too many cats spoils the peace.

Having made the decision to go ahead we decided that we wanted a good pedigree, modern style Siamese to complete the trio, so we searched for some time for the right breeder. Much to our surprise we found someone who fitted the bill slap in the middle of Bristol. Carl, as he is called, had some gorgeous queens that he mated with high calibre pedigree studs. One of the studs' owners was a charming lady called Lynn Russell, who lives in Wiltshire. Her cat Lennox, pictured below, is the father of the little beauty that we acquired from Karl Samson in Bristol.

If you want a good kitten check out the parents. This is our new girl's dad; one Lennox Spartacus Esq. A grand champion no less and a real gent.

So our new little kitty was "Shipshape and Bristol Fashion" (GCCF name Sansomi Signed and Sealed). We were very impressed with the breeder. All the cats at Karl's house looked well cared for and happy and the kittens were charging about like little hell cats. We were excited, but knew that interesting times lay ahead. In order to help with the process of settling the new girl in, we bought a little kittening pen, so that the adult cats could see and interact with her, but not make actual physical contact. This worked very well and is a tactic that I would recommend to those bringing a new kitten home to join some existing residents.

Our new baby girl, who was and is very beautiful, with the clearest sapphire eyes imaginable, did indeed get some verbal abuse from the two in-situ hooligans. But, as the days passed, the level of aggression reduced and the inspection of the kitten pen by Coco and Leo became more relaxed and less noisy. I hasten to add that Emily, as we called her after the Pink Floyd song, was also quite capable of giving some verbals back and has turned out to be a very feisty character. Indeed, she is now undoutedly the boss cat and can strike terror into Leo, who is twice her size. On reflection, Boadicia (Boudica) or Maggie might have been a better name for her.

The new girl, Emily, just letting Mum know that breakfast is late yet again. Little did we know, but we had acquired a tyrant who would rule with a rod of iron.

Social Introductions

After about two weeks we let Emily out of the pen and after a bit of hissing and spitting a more polite form of introduction gradually ensued. Coco made friends with Emily first and clearly held the view that arguing and fighting was all a bit exhausting and got in the way of more important activities, like eating and snoozing. Leo took a bit longer (he is, after all, completely potty) but soon all three were grooming each other and lying together on the sofas and arm chairs dotted around the house. Emily also soon learned to join in the steeplechase and made the cacophony even louder. **Emily is also fast**; indeed in my opinion the world's first jet-powered cat. As readers will know, the modern Siamese is a creature comprised almost entirely of muscle and sinew and, although slight, is extremely powerful for its size. One of Emily's little party tricks, if she is sitting on a bed or a chair, is to leap in the air, complete a 180 degree turn and then exit the room at about 100mph. She looks as though she has been shot out of a cannon; a quite incredible display.

As we got to know Emily she gave us endless fun and pleasure in the high energy antics that she exhibited. A positive life force had definitely been unleashed in the Lawrence household. Even my sons, who are not especially cat people, were smitten. A bundle of fur and muscle, hurtling across the floor and up the curtains was a regular sight. But kittens do exert a toll and a good deal of patience is required.

One of the new girl's less adorable behaviours as a kitten was her way of seeking a cuddle. If she wanted to be held close she would run full tilt at the victim and then climb up his or her legs to the stomach or chest at great speed. But of course the crampons of this little mountaineer were her claws. And wearing shorts, as I sometimes did, meant claws ripping into bare skin. For Benita it was worse, for as she normally wears skirts it meant that flesh was always available and exposed for this excruciating experience. Another of Emily's little tricks, when seeking attention, would be to jump on some unsuspecting person's back and then climb from behind onto the shoulder. She used to do this to me when I was at my desk in the study. If I was deeply engrossed in something and hadn't spotted her this would make me jump out of my skin. Sometimes we would sit down in the evening and inspect our injuries. I used to tell visitors it was the rose bushes or the Pyracantha. Benita, who is much braver than I am about pain, looked like she had come back from a war zone. But we kept our cool, knowing that the feline firebrand would calm down; eventually!

Thankfully, after about a year, these kitten behaviours were history. Benita could wear skirts again and only old scar tissue remains. I could sit at the computer without fearing that a whirling dervish would land on my back. But yes, as the Tovey's often reflected, when a new Siamese arrives you do wonder why the madness actually came over you. As Doreen said it's lucky for the Siamese that they are so beautifiul and endearing, which they certainly are. Emily is what would be called in the West Midlands

Emily at around 4 months; not happy about a view of the world through a wire grille. But also missing her new pal Leo who could not be taken outside. The cat house, now gone, was an expensive white elephant.

a "bobby dazzler" and she knows how to play it for all it is worth. As the father of two sons I have never had the experience of spoiling a daughter. So, only with the arrival of Emily, have I experienced the sense of being enthralled to a little princess. If anyone wants to know where I am, they can always find me wrapped around Emily's little finger. I am just glad cost wise that she doesn't need to go to a Swiss Finishing School and that there is no coming out season in Somerset. We just adore her and she epitomises Da Vinci's view that 'every feline, however small, is a masterpiece'.

Coco has had her admirers as well and back in 2010 she had several of her photos published in the UK's top cat magazine. But as we keep reminding her she was rather more svelte back in those days. She ignores us and believes that her cat walk days are far from over. Some of our friends find the cat magazines very amusing. One refers to them as "Hello Magazine for cats". Mind you he is a retired professor.

With three Siamese in the house we believed we might try to utilise the cat run again that had been built for Coco. As Emily was just a kitten we thought she would soon adjust to some time outside. We tried it a few times and we were wrong; she did not like the cat mansion either. I found that I could not stand to hear her plaintive cries from outside the kitchen door. She was more comfortable if Coco joined her, but then Coco screamed the place down. Siamese certainly learn from each other and if it wasn't good enough for Coco, it was the same for Emily.

Generally speaking I think cats just don't like enclosed spaces, escpecially if there is clearly no possible way out. But also in the case of Siamese I am sure that being put outside meant that they thought they were missing something inside the house. We never tried putting Leo in the run as he is virtually impossible to get into a cat box and, if simply picked up, would resist being held very violently. The only time he becomes supine is at the vets' surgery, when having howled like a banshee on the journey, he becomes completely silent as soon as we enter the practice. By squashing himself down into a ball he also has this amazing abilty to make himself look about half his normal size; adding to the image of this pathetic little creature who has been brought to a place of torture against his will. So Leo did not go into the cat house either. It was like one of those Spanish apartment blocks, built speculatively, but never occupied.

The three amigos

As the time passed our trio really did become the three amigos and it has been a joy to watch the fun and games that the threesome engage in. Any fears about acquiring the third Siamese were abated and we just started to enjoy the whole mad experience. The open spaces in the house mean that they can gallop around at top speed, albeit in contrasting styles. Leo lopes along like a small horse, Emily shoots about like a little rocket and is just a blur as she hurtles past, while Coco's shorter legs move at a frantic pace to try and keep up.

However, some of the antics do have a negative side; Leo, as mentioned before, is a carpet scratcher, Coco likes to bite through vertical blinds and Emily, as we have discovered, is adept at removing wall paper. To be honest the upstairs, where they hang out, is looking in a sorry state. The staircase looks like its is covered in an angora sweater and the blinds as though they were installed to provide ventilation. As for the woodchip, it looks like it has been sanded down with a cheese grater. They make a great demolition unit, the three Thai amigos. We are thinking of renting them out as any house that needed stripping down would be completed in record time.

But overall, we are thankful for small mercies, as by and large, they are not furniture scratchers. Mind you, a 19th century oil painting above the piano did mysteriously acquire a scratched out bald spot which we had not spotted; it's been repaired and moved to a safer place! I only noticed recently, but Coco's fetish for sitting

The three amigos, but note Leo does not look quite so overjoyed about family life as the two ladies. Coco is explaining the facts of life to Emily, hence Leo's discomfiture

on my record deck has put scratches on the perspex lid. No worries, a new one is a snip at £120. With Siamese it's definitely best to keep any items of real value well out of harm's way. But where would that be? The top of the kitchen units are about 4ft above the work surface below. Yet Coco spends a lot of time up there. Her leap from below is something to behold; a bit like watching Jo Brand or Dawn French do the high jump. Yes Coco is still growing and has hit 6.75kgs. Our name is mud at the Langford Small Animal Veterinary Practice.

During the winter and spring after Emily's arrival all was well with the Siamese household. Generally Emily seemed to have enriched the life of the other two mature cats and given them a new zest for life. Coco, who had become somewhat sedentary, was now charging around the house again with great gusto, often pursued by the jet powered kitten. Moving from two to three cats has seemingly doubled the pleasure of our Siamese experience. Mind you Coco's new found exuberance was not without its pitfalls. I happen to be one of those old fashioned people that still plays records and I have a nice and rather expensive record deck. One evening, while some Mahler was booming through the house, a terrible screetching and crashing sound emanated from the area where the HiFi is located in the living room.

I mentioned above that Coco likes to sit on the lid of my record deck. Well now she went a paw step further and got onto the record itself. Coco, fascinated by the revolving LP, had jumped onto it to go round and round with the disc. The ensuing noise was horrendous. Foolishly I had left the lid up. For a minute I thought the deck, pick-up arm and disc were a write off. But despite Coco's 6.75kgs of bulk, the kit all survived and miraculously even the LP was still ok, albeit with a little click throughout the second movement. After this kind of experience it is very tempting to scold a cat and express anger, but I have gradually realised over the years that this is a counterproductive approach. You just take a deep breath and count to ten (or 100 with Siamese).

Emily goes flying

In my experience nowhere that one lives is perfect. Somerset has many virtues: the countryside, the open space, the hills, pleasant people who are a nice blend of real country folk and professional workers who commute to Bristol and Bath. But if there is one thing I don't like here it is the way some people drive. I have always been one of these liberally inclined people that believes that driving is over policed. But never before have I lived somewhere that really is minus speed cameras and police surveillance on the roads. Contrary to my previous prejudice about this the Mendip Hills are a boy racer's paradise. Occasionally a mobile camera unit turns up and catches a few OAPs doing 34mph, but the bad guys always seem to get away with it.

The real motoring problem, though, in Somerset is trucks. Somerset has many quarries, cement works, waste disposal landfill sites and, of course, agricultural vehicles. The county also has a number of A roads that are smaller than many typical B roads. On our local main road, HGVs are often driven over the limit and on the narrow bends they come at you on the wrong side of the centre line. It really is quite scary and I began to find myself leaving the house feeling quite apprehensive if I was taking a car. And then one day my worst fears were realised.

One fine August day I had to take Emily to Langford for a check up and jabs. I put her in a cat box in the back of a Landrover SUV and headed off down the A368 towards Langford. At a lovely place called Rickford the road narrows and there is bad negative camber. It's a tight spot if anything is coming the other way. Just as I passed the Rickford turn I saw a large 40 tonner coming towards me. To my horror I realised that he was about 2 feet over the centre line. In retrospect I don't even know if he saw me, or had just lost concentration. But as the seconds stretched out to oblivion I knew that we were going to collide. My only option was to turn the wheel left and go through a substantial hedge into a field. And that was the choice that I made. I yanked the wheel to the left and we careered through bushes and shrubs into the bed of a small stream. As our vehicle came to a halt I felt something catch me on the side of the neck. This was Emily flying through the air in her cage and smashing into the windscreen. In fact in the tension and panic created by the need just to survive and get out of the way of the truck I had forgotten that she was there. I could feel that my neck was bleeding, but my greatest concern was for our little darling girl.

Emily was badly shaken and had a cut on the side of her head, but she was ok. I was shaking with rage against the driver who had done this to us. I didn't have a reg number, but I did see the name of the haulage company that owned the truck. I phoned and had a good rant at the police and also called the haulage firm and spoke to the boss's wife. She was actually very supportive and apologetic, but pointed out that ultimately it would be my word against the truckers in any legal dispute. And also this was basically what the police said. I calmed down and rang my local garage, who came and towed us out and took me back home. It cost about £1,500 to fix my vehicle, but in many ways I was surprised how well it had withstood the detour into the field.

My injuries and those of Emily soon healed, but I remain very angry about what happened because the same incident could occur again at any time. Our village is supposed to have a 7.5 ton limit on HGVs, but it is not enforced. Road haulage seems to be one of those sectors that can do more or less what it wants. I often discuss the issue with my gardener, who is an ex-policeman. He tries to re-assure me that if you go South it gets even worse. I have vowed not to go South!

Siamese support team

With both Benita and myself working and travelling to France frequently, it's been important to have some good help and support with the cats. In this respect we have been very lucky, and moreover, by pure chance our support team has also given us more links to Doreen Tovey. Pauline Furber, an old friend of Doreen's and also a Siamese breeder who provided some of Doreen's cats, beginning with Saska, has been our great guide and adviser on all matters Siamese. She has also become a great friend to Benita and a regular visitor to our Siamese madhouse. Pauline, a petite blonde with dazzling blue eyes, is always a voice of calm when we go overboard about some Siamese crisis.

She has also been most kind in providing us with extensive materials and information about Doreen, including Doreen's personal diaries. These are invaluable to me, as I am now planning to write a fully-fledged biography of Doreen Tovey. But mostly we are indebted to Pauline for providing some objectivity and sense when we have succombed to some neurosis or other about the cats. Recently, she helped me convince Benita that they did not actually

97

have to have bottled water and that Leo would probably survive without organic chicken; free range has proved good enough. Pauline, who had not bred Siamese for many years, has just started again and her blue-point girl, Tina, has just produced some delightful kittens. She will now have a posse of Siamese charging around her house. Maybe for a while we will be providing the counselling.

Another key part of our support system is the wonderful Clark family, who live in our village. Again by sheer chance it has turned out that Mike Clark was also a friend of Doreen's and, particularly in her later years, Mike chauffered Doreen to and from appointments and also helped her maintain the two acres of garden at the White Cottage. Mike is our very own version of "Father Adams", a larger than life village character who appears in some of the early books. Perhaps unusually for a hard bitten country man, Mike is absolutely potty about cats, as was Father Adams, who owned a female Siamese called Mimi. Mike has a giant-sized Maine Coon, also called Leo, that he adores, but he also looks after our oriental trio when we are away. With Leo almost impossible to get into a cat box, the use of a cattery is out of the question. So the three amigos stay at home and Mike and his wife, Mary, come in to see to their every need. Like Father Adams before him, Mike refers to all animals as males and will often say to us "he's a good-un, that Coco". I reply, "yes, *she* is Mike" and Mike repeats, "Yeh, he's a real goodun".

Mike and his son, Nick, who is a carpenter, built our very grand cat house. It causes us considerable guilt that it is not used as they are always asking if the trio have spent any time outside enjoying the fresh air. We keep making excuses, but we will have to come clean and admit that they are spoiled children who will not go out.

The Clarks are the kindest and most gentle of people and tend to believe that everyone and evverything is equally as benign. They think that Coco (who Mike adores) would get on famously with their Maine Coon, Leo, but we are not so sure. Leo, now about

10kgs in weight, is not a cat to trifle with. He likes to play with Benita and is prone to give her a good nip on the ankles, when she visits. We have decided that the Siamese lady and the boy from Maine will just have to remain penpals.

Leo Clark, the Maine Coon, looking like butter wouldn't melt here, but prone to give you a good nip on the ankles. Coco is opposed to any caternization.

9

A Crisis with Leo

Sometimes, when life is going well, I feel that I should pinch myself to check that it is real. I am, in short, a worrier. I often recall one of my former bosses at university who used to say that, 'a pessimist is just a better informed optimist'. I would say in addition, 'cherish the good times, because they don't last'. After Emily's arrival everything was going swimmingly, life had become utterly idyllic. Stressful moves and annoying neighbours were things of the past. But my forebodings were well founded. It was indeed too good to be true; trouble was just around the corner.

Our period of domestic bliss, in our lovely village with the cats, came to an end in the Spring of 2013, when Leo became seriously ill. A medical crisis during the life of a cat is quite likely, but typically at a later age than five. Being Leo, of course, it couldn't be anything

Happy times. Leo and Emily chilling out on the sofa.

simple to diagnose, or easy to treat. In fact it was difficult to really see any change in his health at all. Benita noticed it at first; telling me that he seemed listless and out of sorts. I was rather complacent about the situation, thinking that he had picked up some bug or minor infection. This had happened with Lucky once and he just took to his bed for a couple of days and was then as right as rain. But Leo's lethargy continued and I was forced to concede that something was wrong. So we took him down (after the normal manic battle to get him into a catbox) to the Bristol University Small Animal Practice at Lanford, which we are very fortunate to have right on our doorstep. The practice is part of the University of Bristol Veterinary School and has world class facilities and staff who specialise in felines. As well as the small animal practice surgery, Langford has a small animal hospital, where major surgery can be conducted and first class residential after care is available. If your pet is unfortunate enough to become seriously ill, this is one of the best places in Europe for treatment. The Toveys were regular visitors to Langford, frequently dashing from Rowberrow down the A38 to take any poorly Siamese for treatment.

Major surgery

I was expecting Leo's consultation to yield nothing too serious, but after an extensive examination the vet on duty expressed the view that Leo may have pancreatitus; an infection of the pancreas, with potentially dangerous implications. Leo then remained at the practice for a couple of days for further tests and was in fact discovered, not to have pancreatitus, but rather to be suffering from a blocked bile duct, linked to a nasty condition called cholangitis, essentially an infection of the bile duct. So yes, the boy from Bangkok had come up trumps with a real medical cracker.

Cholangitis in cats is a very rare condition and not easy to treat. The prognosis is also not good, especially as many cats are only brought for examination when they are quite ill. As I have said it is very easy to miss the initial symptoms. At least with Leo we had not made that mistake. He was "under the weather" as they say, but not at death's door. Further analysis of Leo's blockage revealed that it actually consisted of the e-coli bacterium and it needed to be removed for him to have a real chance of recovery. By now readers will know that Leo is a nervy, neurotic and reclusive cat who hates to be handled and really doesn't like people, other than his owners. So on top of the medical condition there was the fact that he was massively stressed by the experience of being in captivity. The poor little mite was endlessly tested and examined and generally had a hellish time, despite being treated with the greatest of care.

After several protracted and sometimes tense discussions it was agreed, with the team at the hospital linked to the practice, that Leo would need major surgery. We were mortified by this news and discussions with the surgeon were not always easy. We vacillated from one view to another and could not make up our mind. We wanted an unavailable solution that avoided major surgery. And there was also more bad news. It was very scary for us to learn that there would be a 5% risk of mortality during or after the procedure. This is, of course, for anyone rational, also a 95% chance of survival, so it really is a case of whether the glass is 5% empty or 95% full? But we were in real panic mode and oblivious to risk statistics.

We were beside ourselves with worry. On reflection I think that Benita and I were also in utter denial about the bad news. And as we were not really willing to face the facts, discussions with the surgeon were tense and difficult. We really were shooting the messenger. He had simply been straight and direct with us which, in my experience, is the way surgeons normally play it. And he was right; ultimately we knew deep down that the surgical medical intervention was essential and for Leo's own good. Contrary to my old boss's advice, we tried to be optimistic and imagine Leo happy and well again.

But in these situations there is also an issue about what one should put an animal through, especially a very nervous and frightened one. We had let Lucky undertake chemotherapy at the age of 15 and, looking back, believed that to be a bad decision. Although it was over four years since Lucky had died, it only seemed like yesterday. We tearfully and repeatedly asked ourselves: were we really going to lose Leo as well?

Eventually sense prevailed and we realised that it was a very different situation from the one with Lucky. In Leo's case, with him being only 5 years old, we thought that the invasive treatment was justified and that it was best to accept Langford's advice. However, we had still not agreed a date. Then, one Sunday afternoon at home, watching Leo listlessly mooching about, it became clear that he was getting worse. He seemed exhausted and was not eating (even chicken). I got him into his cat box, with little resistance as he was so weak, and I took him down to the animal hospital. I was told that I would be met by the head of neuro science, who was the vet on duty for that weekend.

The day of reckoning

After I pulled up at Langford I got out of the car and took Leo to the front double doors of the hospital, which were locked. It was one of those really blustery April days in the West of England when the wind blows hard and dark clouds scud rapidly across the sky, bringing violent, squally showers. Leo looked in a sorry state, cowering in his basket by the doors. I was having a good fret, when suddenly a young chap turned up to let us in. I thought he was a student from the Veterinary School, as he looked about 19. To my astonishment he explained that he was the head of Neurology, freshly arrived from Cambridge. He then explained that he had come to Somerset, as he and his wife preferred the West of the country to East Anglia and that he especially enjoyed the fishing.

He made me feel about 100 years old; this charming young man who had obviously progressed so quickly in his career. I decided that I had met the Professor Brian Cox of Veterinary Science. I was sure that he must have been a child prodigy, someone who had gone to

103

university at 13 and then married at 16. He reminded me of the young actor who had played Dougy Howser in the 1980s series about a teenage hospital doctor in the US. But anyway, coming back to reality, I saw that he was taking Leo upstairs and I followed him to a consulting room, where he gave Leo a quick lookover. I still could not entirely believe that he was not a second year student, but his confidence, charm and obvious professional skills soon convinced me. After Leo's examination it was decided that he should remain at Langford, with the "op" pencilled in for Tuesday.

But this was not routine small animal surgery and we were so fortunate to have specialist expertise so close to hand. The surgeon was going to have to make a full length incision along the abdomen and take a number of biopsy samples and then flush through the bile duct and remove the obstruction, which, as said before, turned out to be e-coli. This was a very difficult procedure requiring great skill, as the diameter of the bile duct in a cat is tiny.

On the day of the operation neither of us could really focus on anything and we simply waited in stressed-out limbo for news. I went shopping to a nearby town to try and distract myself, but it was an unsuccessful tactic. The hours dragged on and there was no news. In fact, it turned out that Leo had gone in for his surgery much later than anticipated. We were worrying how it had gone even before the operation had started. We were both at home just waiting, with the minutes ticking away at snail's pace. Then about 7pm the phone rang. I picked up the receiver in a kind of trance and spoke to Pete Hogg, the chief clinician at Langford. It was good news; the procedure was definitely successful and had gone as well as could possibly be hoped. We were incredibly relieved, but also had to endure a tense wait of a few days to see if there was any internal rupture or infection. But all was well again and our little terrified and nervous boy survived and, after a week's recuperation on a special cat ward, came back to us. Albeit looking in a sorry state. Although there is always a comic side.

Leo had been fed nutrients and fluids through a tube in his neck. This was because with no roast chicken available he had gone on hunger strike. So the staff at Langford had put a narrow white bandage around the neck area, over the incision wound. Bizarrely this looked just like a vicar's white collar. With Leo being all black he looked like some kind of feline priest. I half expected him to start saying "amen", when we gave him his dinner; he did look very comical. In fact he had lost a great deal of his coat and seemed like a crossed sphynx, the strange but now popular breed that has no fur at all.

Leo, about 3 weeks after his surgery. By this time the vicar's collar had gone, but he still had lots of missing fur. Cats are resilient and he soon recovered.

Normality restored

We were hugely impressed with the staff at Langford and particularly with the chief clinician and surgeon, who both did a wonderful job. We were the ones who were not easy to deal with and, as I have said, we did not want to accept that Leo had a life threatening condition. Leo, after a shaky first week post the operation, has gone from strength to strength. Indeed, it soon became clear to us retrospectively that he had been quite unwell in the weeks prior to the surgery, as the new post-surgery Leo was much livelier and more energetic than the poor boy who went to hospital back in April. Indeed, he's started playing football again and throwing dental chews up in the air and leaping like a bucking bronco to catch them.

For the most part Leo handled the crisis very well, which must have been very difficult for him as he is so nervy. But yes, old "wriggle bum", as the Langford staff called him, came through. In many ways the most troubling aspect of the episode is how we rather went to pieces and succumbed to depression and stress. Despite the fact that Leo is not human, Benita and I found the experience extremely traumatic amd upsetting. Human attachment to pets is an extraordinary thing. We realised that our lives, and even our happiness, was utterly entwined with those of the cats. I wondered if it was good to be so wrapped up in the fates of our little Siamese trio? But in reality this was all academic; there was no turning back.

Maybe there is a lesson here about life and love. The obvious downside of love is vulnerabilty to loss. And with animals, such as dogs and cats, having a lifespan about one fifth of ours', some sadness and grief at some point is inevitable. Is it better to have loved and lost? Again, to bring Doreen Tovey back into the story, readers will recall how she and René lost their beloved Seeley when he was about five or six. He did not perish from illness or an accident, but simply disappeared; in my view the worst kind of loss. In the book, Doreen seems remarkably stoical about the tragedy, but in reality we know it must have been a terrible experience. We still think of Seeley when we walk in the valley near Rowberrow and it re-inforces our commitment to keeping our lot inside.

Philosophical reflections aside all that really mattered to us about Leo was that he recovered from the surgery and that the condition did not return. On that score, it was so far so good. The days passed and soon clear signs of improvement were evident. Little by little it seemed that a risk of a major relapse or a rupture was becoming remote. We just wanted everything back to normal.

Leo, restored to health and ready for a spot of petty larceny. He has now taken to running off with our tooth brushes and Benita's underwear!

Gradually, with plenty of TLC from Benita, all was well and Leo seemed fitter than ever and strangely, given his traumatic experience, rather less neurotic and skittish than before his major surgery and fortnight in hospital. Maybe he now thinks that after his trip to *Alcatraz* nothing worse could ever befall him. A new habit that has emerged with Leo post surgery demands a mention here. We are not sure if the root cause of this is that Leo has become house proud, or, if it is the result of some strange fetish. Knowing him as we do, it is more likely to be the latter.

Leo has decided that he does not like to see any clothes drying on radiators. Although it is not very prepossessing, I must confess that in the winter certain garments are left to dry on radiators at Chez Lawrence. Typically tea towels, tops, socks and underwear. Certainly some of Benita's more fetching under garments are on display, if we know that no one is due at the house. But Leo Stringfellow doesn't like it, and, as soon as our backs are turned, all washing, especially little frilly items, are pulled onto the floor. And I don't mean just one or two, Leo scours the house to make sure that all radiators are clear. Maybe he gets a premonition about when the Rector is due to call. But, for whatever reason, he takes the clothes down. I wonder if Arnold Layne, Pink Floyd's lady's underwear thief, could be another nickname for this mad cat. He has also taken a shine to our electric toothbrushes. These are put on to re-charge in the bedroom in a socket at floor level and Leo clamps them in his mouth and runs off with the brushes. It's not really doing any harm. Other than the fact that there are tooth marks on the handles.

There is also another downside with his new and more confident personality. Leo has always had a voice like a foghorn. It is not a miaow, more a whaoaha; sometimes very deep and guttural, at others times high pitched and wailing. But now, post operation, the volume sems to have increased about 20 decibels. In the evening, just before bedtime, Leo outlines to Benita, in the clearest and loudest terms, his requirement for a roast chicken supper. This involves him positioning himself in the kitchen and screaming whaoaha, whaoaha, whaaoha with increasing volume and frequency until the chicken arrives. In fact he is becoming a real bully. If we are in the living room watching TV and not providing a fast enough service he comes in and ups the volume to the point where it is unbearable. Sometimes in novelty shops or at cat shows one sees mugs or little plaques with humorous comments about being bossed about by cats. A popular one is, "Dogs have masters, Cats have staff". But this is no longer a joke in our house. Benita, who loves Leo dearly, is getting fed up with this and has started to utter a counter narrative to the effect of "shut your trap". But I know who will fall silent first.

10

War and Peace

It was wonderful having Leo back. We both felt a profound sense of relief that he was ok. But there was a strange, unwelcome and unanticipated downside to Leo's return. When Leo came home Benita decided that he needed to be isolated from the other cats, as any wild romps or play fights could have opened his wound or risked internal rupture. I can say that in all honesty I was against this policy, but the boss of cats overuled me. And I could see the logic of Benita's argument; we didn't want him back at Langford.

Siamese strife

When Leo returned to normal contact with the rest of the household he was fine with Coco, but very hostile and aggressive to Emily. Emily responded in kind and began chasing Leo around the house with her tail bushed out in battle mode. At first we believed that this was possibly because of the strange smells and odours that Leo may have brought back from the hospital, but as time went on it was as though they had forgotten each other. Any meetings resulted in growling, spitting and even blows being struck, but thankfully no biting. The fighting was mainly posturing, but tended to escalate if we did not intervene. We had a cat war on our hands.

This was a novel situation for us and we hoped that after a few weeks we would see the end of this liitle war, but it endured. We were mortified, but obviously determined to find a solution. We began to devour everything that we could find to read in books and on the web on cat behaviour. We even contacted the famous behaviourist, Peter Neville, to ask for advice. He was most helpful and put us in touch with a charming lady in Devon, who specialised in this kind of cat problem. This lovely lady, Rachel, even came up to Somerset to see the protagonists in situ. She gave us advice and a programme of action for a gradual re-introduction. She also made it clear that we would have to be patient; these spats could endure.

In the meantime we have had to re-organise our household on the lines of the two Koreas or maybe the Greek and Turkish Cyprus model. Coco and Leo still get on well and clearly the bonds established by the length of their relationship have proved stronger than the impact of temporary separation. They could roam the house and play, eat and sleep together with no problems. While Leo was out and about in the house Emily stayed in her room. Then we would put Leo in his room for few a hours and Emily came out to see Coco. It was a little like a timeshare rota where the diferent tenants use the same space, but never meet. Fortunately, Coco and Emily have remained the best of friends and they now sleep in one room upstairs and Leo in another. Yes! Our cats now occupy two different bedrooms in their suite upstairs.

Therapy

The feline therapy consists mainly of a gradual re-introduction process. After about a month we started allowing Emily to enter Leo's lair. He darted under the bed and began to hiss and growl at Little Em, as we now call her. Emily's response has been very interesting; she rolls on her back, wiggles about and makes come hither noises to old grumpy drawers. So it is very clear who the aggressor is. Emily will then often jump on top of Leo's bed and stay in the room for an hour or so. He tolerates this and remains under the bed sulking. But overtime the spitting and hissing has died down. We also tried re-introducing the kitten pen and putting Emily inside it at the bottom of the stairs. But old Mr. Reclusive just stayed in his room and Emily hated being in the pen, so this tactic failed.

With Emily staying in Leo's room for hours on end we thought that we were making real progress. However, when Leo appeared from under the bed there was still some aggression, albeit muted and thankfully with no real or damaging violence. At this point Coco would appear, clearly very fed up with Leo, and give him a few sharp Siamese words, but not actually get involved in the spat. Emily's tail would be splayed out about 3 inches, which looks very strange on a tiny, little female cat. The mighty atom has stabilised at a very trim 3 kgs, but still stands her ground against Leo, who weighs over 6 kgs.

Time passed and we persisted with this approach and gradually it did start to pay dividends. Although not before the whole daft episode meant that Coco and Emily ended up in Langford. We took our eyes off the ball, as they say. As my old boss would have said, we succumbed to ill-informed optimism.

Back to Langford

On one particular Saturday morning Emily and Leo seemed to be getting on much better and we took the risk of popping out to the

A flashback to happier times with the trio. Although Coco looks rather fed up with the other two. She is always the balanced and sensible one.

shops for an hour or so, while leaving them both out in the house. When we got back home, all hell had seemingly been let loose. Coco looked utterly traumatised, Emily's tail was about a foot wide and Leo was howling and screaming. There had obviously been a big bust up. We checked them all for any injuries and, to our relief, found that there were no puncture wounds and no signs of any blood. Seemingly, then, it had just been a big screaming match. But it was clear that leaving the cats out together in the house had been premature. We would have to rebuild again from scratch.

Coco and Little Em; still the best of pals but rattled and upset about the fight with Leo

Sunday passed uneventfully, but with Coco and Emily hiding away. By Monday morning it was very clear that Coco and Emily were still upset and they were not eating. In Coco's case this was very worrying, as she really does like her grub. So the female cats were basketed up and taken off to Langford. By and large the staff over there are delightful people, but there is one rather fierce female vet and she gave me a real dressing down for letting the little spat take place and ignoring all the behavioural pointers. For good measure she also gave me a good ear wigging over Coco's weight. I felt like a naughty boy who had been sent before the Head Mistress. Then she alarmed me by saying that she wanted to keep Coco and Emily at the surgery for observation.

A few hours later I received a call from this formidable lady vet informing me that she was 'very worried' about Coco and that she (Coco) was in real danger. I was shocked and horrified. We had gone from what I thought was a mildly troubling situation of a cat going off its food, to a serious prognosis of a life threatening condition in about three hours. But it turned out that the problem was rooted in a big paradox at work in the medical scenario that had arisen. Coco really was in danger.

As the feline lady in question is very well upholstered, to say the least, I had thought that a few days off the pie and chips might do no harm at all. But in fact, as I discovered to my horror, a cat that is very overweight is at significant rsk of liver damage if it stops eating. Unlike many other animals, who can safely go without food for a long period of time, cats cannot. If a cat stops eating or her normal daily caloric intake drops dramatically, it's a only a brief period of time before the potentially fatal disease, hepatic lipidosis, attacks the liver. And cats that are overweight are at the greatest risk.

Coco fitted perfectly the profile of a cat most at risk of this disease, as the felines most likely to succumb to hepatic lipidosis, also known as fatty liver syndrome, are middle-aged, overweight cats that have recently lost a considerable amount of weight. The condition is caused because the cat's body, deprived of sufficient calories, sends large numbers of fat cells to the liver to be converted into energy. However, cat's bodies aren't designed to metabolize fat in this way, so the buildup of fat cells undermines liver function; a potentially fatal situation. We were worried sick, with the only bright spot being that at least Emily was allowed back home.

Emily, safely back from Langford, but missing her big pal Coco. Emily was less at risk from hepatic lipidosis because of her svelte, slim figure.

When this information had sunk in Benita and I agreed that Coco could be fed by tube and kept in overnight for observation. But it was all very upsetting, especially as we had only just nursed Leo back to health. Thankfully, Coco came home the next day and soon started eating again. She looked very odd though, as some kind of tube had been secured across the top of her head with sticky tape. After we removed the tape the fur was still pressed down and stuck together in clumps by a gluey residue, which we couldn't remove. In the end we had to cut the fur off to get rid of the glue and poor Coco looked as though she had alopecia and also as though something had flattened the top of her head. Coco is pretty laid back normally, but this business had really got on her nerves and we were given a right tongue lashing by the Wokingham belle. But business is business for Coco and she soon got back to normal eating and was put on a controlled diet that is having some success. I don't want another dressing down by the fierce vet from Langford and I am determined that Coco will trim down.

Coco, on the mend after her trauma at Langford. This is her lioness pose.
But the pounds have to come off!

Peace treaty?

With a few more months gone by it seems that relations are now on the mend. It's all been rather sad for us, as the three amigos became so estranged. However, the three are now spending longer spells out in the house with no real problems, apart from Leo growling. Nevertheless, it shows how serious these behavioural problems with cats can be, as 6 months later the problem is still not entirely resolved. But the day is clearly approaching when we can abandon the two cat households solution and go back to normality. The gradual re-introduction programme is now clearly working, but has been a long and slow process.

This problem is called by behaviourists "lack of recognition" aggression and can happen because cats have quite short memories and literally forget each other. Although, obviously Leo did not forget Coco, who he had known for much longer. Emily must have been confused by the strange hospital odours and smells that Leo

115

brought back from Langford. Doubtless, the fact that they are Siamese "moderns" and basically bonkers made it more difficult to resolve than if they were more normal cats. Leo and Emily are both "moderns" and very similar in temperament. Although Leo is more skittish. We also wonder if, ideally, Leo would like to be a solitary cat. He is certainly a unique individual; what the French would call "special".

Cats at court

As winter begins here in Somerset we are definitely getting back to normal and one of our old rituals with the cats has recommenced. Thinking about it makes me realise again that Siamese cats are remarkable animals. One of their little foibles is that they like to sit with us and take their ease in the evening, as though we are at court. Before dinner we often relax in a small sitting room just off the kitchen. Coco and Emily sit at our backs on the top of the sofa and Leo in front, under a coffee table. No one does anything, Benita and I just sit there and chat companiably, while the cats watch. We then have dinner and reconvene afterwards in the main living room. The trio follow us in and the process is repeated. Leo sits on the sofa watching TV, while the ladies sit on the floor or sometimes on top of the piano.

This scenario remains peaceful and relaxing until about 9:30pm, when Coco begins a process of agitation to secure supper and go to bed. This starts with low level provocations and will culminate in her walking on the mantle piece around ornaments or jumping onto the HiFi. Another tactic, if this doesn't work, is climbing inside the TV unit and messing with the wires. The only way to stop it is to get up and provide food and put the two girls to bed. Leo then gets half an hour on his own with his mistress, which is clearly his *me time*. His relationship with Benita is extraordinary; he follows her around the house like a little dog. When she returns from work in the evening, just the sound of the car will bring him running full tilt to the back door. What it is to be loved!

Farewell from Somerset

As the time ticks on into real winter all is now well in the Siamese household (we humans are just here to keep house). Coco is still the Epicurean Duchess, sleeping a lot and stealing food at every opportunity and Emily continues to accelerate around the house like a turbo-charged electron. Today a man has been to measure up for new carpets. The previous ones have lasted a year; quite good by Siamese standards. We have gradually learned to accept the drawbacks of the Siamese regime. As I sit here writing a last few words I can hear Leo pulling at the stair carpet, Coco is in the window chewing the vertical blinds and Emily is resting in her bedroom, before she is let out onto the landing to have another scratch at the wall paper. Relations continue to improve and we seem to have the three amigos back. Such is optimism and happiness in a Siamese corner of Somerset.

About the Author

Philip Lawrence is a writer, consultant and freelance journalist specialising in aerospace and defence. He has contributed regularly to the *Financial Times, Wall Steet Journal* and a number of European publications, such as Cinco Dias and Europe's World. He has published 8 previous books including:

Preparing for Armageddon, (Wheatsheaf Press, 1988).
Knowledge and Power, (Avebury, 1996).
Stratgeic Trade in Commercial Class Aircraft, (Chatham House, 1998*).*
Modernity and War, (Macmillan, 1999).
Deep Stall, (Ashgate, 2005).

Cats in Charge is Philip's first venture into what he hopes will be considered humorous writing.